ELIZABETH MURRAY: PAINTINGS AND DRAWINGS

ELIZABETH MURRAY:

Organized by Sue Graze and Kathy Halbreich

With Essay by Roberta Smith

and Notes by Clifford S. Ackley

PAINTINGS AND DRAWINGS

Harry N. Abrams, Inc., Publishers, New York

In association with the Dallas Museum of Art

and the MIT Committee on the Visual Arts

This publication was prepared on the occasion of the exhibition *Elizabeth Murray: Paintings and Drawings,* organized by Sue Graze, Curator of Contemporary Art, Dallas Museum of Art, and Kathy Halbreich, former Director of the Albert and Vera List Visual Arts Center, Massachusetts Institute of Technology.

The organization and national tour of the exhibition have been supported by grants from the National Endowment for the Arts and the Massachusetts Council on the Arts and Humanities.

Exhibition Travel Schedule

March 1–April 19, 1987
Dallas Museum of Art, Dallas

May 8–June 28, 1987
Albert and Vera List Visual Arts Center, MIT, Cambridge
Museum of Fine Arts, Boston

July 28–September 20, 1987
The Museum of Contemporary Art, Los Angeles

November 10, 1987–January 3, 1988
Des Moines Art Center, Des Moines

January 31–March 27, 1988
Walker Art Center, Minneapolis

April 21–June 26, 1988
Whitney Museum of American Art, New York

Editor: Edith M. Pavese
Designer: Samuel N. Antupit

Library of Congress Cataloging-in-Publication Data
Murray, Elizabeth, 1940–
   Elizabeth Murray, paintings and pastels.
   Exhibition organized by the Dallas Museum of Art and the Albert and Vera List Visual Arts Center, Massachusetts Institute of Technology.
   Bibliography: p. 135
   Includes index.
   1. Murray, Elizabeth, 1940–   —Exhibitions. I. Graze, Sue. II. Halbreich, Kathy. III. Smith, Roberta. IV. Ackley, Clifford S. V. Dallas Museum of Art. VI. Albert and Vera List Visual Arts Center.
N6537.M87A4 1987 759.13 86-17297
ISBN 0-8109-1423-9

Times Mirror Books   Printed and bound in Japan

CONTENTS

FOREWORD

Elizabeth Murray holds a unique position in contemporary American art. Her ability to seize the formal issues present in the art of our time and to integrate those with the psychic and emotional side of everyday life distinguishes her work.

Elizabeth Murray has created art that speaks of honesty, courage, and a willingness to take risks. In giving artistic expression to today's highly complex world, she is, like the scientist, constantly forging new territory. It is these qualities which initially captured the attention of both the Dallas Museum of Art and the Massachusetts Institute of Technology and brought these seemingly disparate institutions together in a collaborative effort to present the first major exhibition and book of Elizabeth Murray's artistic development over the past ten years.

Throughout the planning and organization of this exhibition, Sue Graze, Curator of Contemporary Art of the Dallas Museum of Art, and Kathy Halbreich, until recently Director of the Albert and Vera List Visual Arts Center at MIT, have shown extraordinary care and commitment and it is their vision that we share with you today.

Moreover, it is a measure of the respect and enthusiasm for Elizabeth Murray that so many lenders have been willing to share works from their collections, and we are deeply grateful for that support. We also wish to acknowledge and thank those sister institutions who are participants in this exhibition's tour, notably the Museum of Fine Arts, Boston; The Museum of Contemporary Art, Los Angeles; the Des Moines Art Center; the Walker Art Center; and the Whitney Museum of American Art.

It is with great respect and admiration that we celebrate the achievements of this outstanding artist.

Harry S. Parker III, Director,
Dallas Museum of Art

Paul E. Gray, President,
Massachusetts Institute of Technology

WHAT IT IS

More than you know me there is
    Something in my eye. Is it
A volcano? I mean window. I mean,
Excuse me, are you talking to me?
I brought you something, but you
Came through it so at least everything
Will be different, starting immediately.
Difficulty is your daughter, too, she adds.
Vast apples! How sorry the sorry image,
Romanticism cubed. That is the question:
Forget it! Now, slowly remove propeller
From tuba, gently stretching umbilical
Accordion to full spectrum—that's it.
Your move. Your witness. Yours truly.

Bob Holman
1985

MOTION PICTURES

Elizabeth Murray's art has always been in motion and about motion. This sums up both the restless nature of her development and the belief at the center of her work: that a painting is essentially an event, an animation of form that sets the viewer's thoughts and feelings in motion. At first, we may not know exactly what is going on in one of Murray's paintings, but the feeling of something happening is undeniable. We are pulled in by the sense of objects and space on the move, of color and painted and literal shapes subject to various internal and external pressures. Everything is in flux, is undergoing a process of change and distortion that is visually strange and abstract, but also psychologically real, and we enter into the process too.

A Murray painting usually confronts you with an enticing surface dominated by strong colors and inventive shapes, a surface that is applied to a clunky, irregularly-shaped, overtly hand-built canvas-stretcher hybrid. For several years now, Murray's paintings have been pushed eccentrically off square, fragmented into mini-canvases that sometimes overlap or are wedged together, or appended with additional shaped canvases that may jut aggressively outward. To literally see Murray's image means contending with this barrage of three-dimensional information. And just when you've located the point—in space and in your own mind—where the physical and the visual seem reconciled, the painting's possible meanings start coming out at you too, requiring you to reconcile the physical and visual forms with the narrative they are communicating.

Murray's forms, like her surfaces, are savvy and eclectic, touching on the major abstract efforts of the twentieth century, updating and energizing them with, among other things, a thoroughly American love of cartooning, fusing them into a fairly seamless style. Murray will combine some of Gris' shadowed layering of form with Arp's biomorphism in Suprematist deep space and serve it all up with more than a touch of Disney on a scale that is confidently Abstract Expressionist. In contrast to this sophisticated handling of styles, the narrative that often emerges is surprisingly banal and domestic, and sometimes even corny. These events don't show themselves immediately. They're almost always helped along by Murray's cryptic titles: *More Than You Know, Can You Hear Me?, Her Story, Yikes, Just in Time, Not Goodbye*. But gradually her buoyant, self-assured abstractions reveal themselves to be visual amplifications, writ large, of the minor accidents and private exchanges that fuel everyday life. The flying forms in Murray's paintings frequently turn out to be topsy-turvy coffee cups and saucers or goblets spilling their contents, or big pneumatic hands grasping equally inflated paintbrushes (or phalluses). A gyrating chair or an unusually palpable beam of light may be the main protagonist. A vaguely figural cloud or attenuated Gumby-person may sail through space, sometimes accompanied by a piece of furniture. Implied emotional pressures—children's plaints, lovers' retorts, unexpected confessions—abound, as does a sense of intimate relationships spinning out of control. And invariably, an event that is merely domestic, intensely personal, or completely subconscious seems to assume cataclysmic proportions before our eyes.

Obviously, a painting by Elizabeth Murray is a visual and mental handful—pleasurable yet irritating, aggressive yet multi-layered and elusive. Likewise, Murray's development and her achievement as a whole are not easy to encapsulate. Hers is a sensibility of many parts and developmental phases; and it fits into several locales in the landscape of contemporary art without coming completely to rest anywhere.

Murray is an inveterate story teller, for whom subject matter, conveyed by the appropriate form, is all. "The subconscious is what you paint about," she says. Like many of the best so-called Neo-Expressionists', Murray's is an art of primal emotions; sometimes the formative psychological moments she portrays are as charged and specific as those in Eric Fischl's or Francesco Clemente's paintings. Like many of the Neo-Expressionists, she has also made extensive use of past art; like Julian Schnabel in particular she is an American artist with a decidedly European side to her sensibility. And Murray has certainly evolved her own version of the fractured, collage-like synthesis of disparate parts so prevalent in the 1980s.

Murray is also a dedicated formalist. She has assiduously articulated all of painting's basic elements—paint, surface, and support—as rigorously, if not so exclusively, as Robert Ryman. In her work the physical facts of building a stretcher and making a painting play an active role in the final image, both extending and checking its highly illusive space and highly allusive narrative. Since the late 1970s in particular, Murray has participated in what might be called the post-formalist rejuvenation, or repsychologizing of abstract painting. (This endeavor has involved artists from various countries and generations, among them Frank Stella, Sigmar Polke, Gerhard Richter, Howard Hodgkin, Brice Marden, Gary Stephan, Judy Pfaff, Terry Winters, and Carroll Dunham.) The primary aspects of this revitalization, all evident in Murray's work, include the reactivation of pictorial space, an emphasis on legibility and subject matter, and, at times, a tendency toward an eye-boggling degree of "complexity and contradiction" (to quote Robert Venturi). Inspired in part by Neo-Expressionism, it would seem, contemporary abstraction has started talking back to the viewer with a new kind of consciousness—about life, art history, popular culture, its own intricate physical nature. This consciousness uses the self-referential, self-reflexive stance of modernism as a basis for a greatly expanded sense of self for both artist and viewer alike.

Murray's ability to be counted in both the "abstract" and "Neo-Expressionist" camps is a tribute to her achievement and also one more indication of the dwindling distinction between abstraction and representation overall—in itself perhaps the most important development in art since 1970. Still, her art doesn't settle completely into either camp. Abstract painters who admire her inventive shapes are often made uneasy by what they actually turn out to depict. And Murray, unlike Susan Rothenberg, has never been accepted as "one of the guys" by the Neo-Expressionists—or their enthusiastic curators. In both cases, this may be because Murray's art has evolved a distinctly feminist character and this earns her membership in a third, equally important "camp."

Along with many artists her age and younger, Murray is part of what might be called the de-genderization of art, which has been pushed forward on many fronts and in various media since the early 1970s, gaining force as it goes. Much of this effort has, understandably, been conducted outside painting, in photography and photo-related work, where male domination of the medium is not so entrenched. Subverting from within, Murray has helped re-work abstract painting from a specifically non-male point of view. Her development has been a process of progressively taking on the most persistent issues of modernism—flatness, figure-ground, illusion, the physical support—in order to deal with feelings that, while not strictly the province of women, are definitely more familiar to women, and she has made these feelings available to everyone.

The figures in Murray's work are non-male human presences whose streamlined forms are part of the history of twentieth-century art and American popular culture both, and whose emotions are equally modern and ambiguous. In her best and most recent work, Murray frequently touches on a kind of craziness which conventionally has been thought of as "female." Her art repeatedly and subtly argues that it is a craziness that we all, men and women alike, experience, and that such emotions originate in the first few years of life, before society's process of sexual differentiation sets in. With a strange combination of humor and genuine empathy, Murray deals with the violence of these intense emotions in ways that are deliberately disembodied and nongendered, explicitly spatial and abstract. In essence, Murray has developed an uncanny ability to convert emotional pressures into formal ones, allowing their urgency to warp first her shapes, then her space, and, finally, the very surfaces upon which she works.

Perhaps the history of the art of the past fifteen years is also one of pressures, the story of a series of irresistible forces acting upon the old, immovable objects of New York-based modernism. These pressures include feminism, regionalism, popular culture, psychological and historical subject matter, as well as the unfinished business of European modernism itself. If so, few careers personify these pressures as clearly, as richly, and as presciently as Murray's. Born in Chicago and educated there and in the San Francisco area, Murray spent nearly a decade making art that was fiendishly regional, simplistically feminist, rife with cartoon imagery and psychological melodrama before she came to New York and began to contend with the legacy of modernism. In short, the irresistible forces which would help form '70s art are part and parcel of her psyche and her background and, until 1971, they run rampant in her work.

When I began to write this essay, the spiral image seemed to be the obvious starting point for a discussion of Murray's achievement. It is ubiquitous to her art: we see it in the curving lines that retrace their paths in ever more generous routes; in the bulbous, genie-like clouds that swirl up from deep space and bob before us; in the exaggerated vanishing points of the space itself and the torqued arrangements of canvases; and, most of all, in the emotional spin that Murray has gradually built into her art. The spiral is basic even to the shape of Murray's development and to the manner in which, on every level, she has pursued her goals, always pushing forward to try something new, yet always reviewing familiar territory from higher, more ambitious ground. When you consider her work from 1972 or '73, when she started to be recognized, she has what might be called a classic '70s artist's career. Like many of her contemporaries, especially Joel Shapiro, Murray seems to have a back-to-basics beginning in which the essential processes of forming, of building and marking on a surface, were at first tentatively, and then with increasing confidence, fused with the processes of signing, of creating a rich symbolic content. Like Shapiro, she then proceeded along an anti-reductivist course, reversing the minimizing tendencies of modernism in general and Minimalism in particular and over the course of the decade moving toward increasing complexities of form and meaning and a broader consciousness in both the psychological and the art historical sense.

It's exciting to think of Murray quietly biding her time, building her art throughout the 1970s to its current pace, but there's more to it. Murray's early '70s art is the first work she is comfortable calling her own, but it is really the middle or second phase of her development. When you take Murray's graduate and "post graduate" work from the '60s into consideration, the whole story turns out to be both simpler and more dramatic: what seems at first a spiral is actually a full circle. Particularly in her work of the '80s, Murray has returned to an idea of pictorial illusionism combined with overt physicality, of abstraction combined with and activated by a suggestive psycho-spatio-domestic narrative, which she had in mind from the very beginning and which she had to disassemble, pare down, and rearrange in order to build up again and get right.

Murray started out in the early '60s working

at her present velocity, with her current ideas of narrative complexity and visual ferociousness largely in place, but the art she made was conventional, unoriginal and frequently close to awful. Until the early '70s, Murray seems to have worked at fever pitch, regularly making and destroying large elaborate works, or series of small ones. Her art from this time conveys a combination of ambition, desperation, and dull familiarity; it tells the story of a painter for whom painting was simply not enough, who continually sought to make the medium more physical, more narrative, and more animated than it usually was.

To this end, and inspired by the examples of Johns, Rauschenberg, and Oldenburg, Murray made an assortment of shaped, cut-out, and cut-up canvases, built out her surfaces with thick paint, appended them with forms made of sewn, often stuffed fabric, and occasionally with parts of furniture. She appropriated cartoon imagery, using Dick Tracy and Little Orphan Annie as points of departure for both painting and writing; she captioned her paintings or made their titles part of the image, as in *Little Orphan Annie on the Beach,* or *Balboa Discovers the Pacific Ocean* (this last forming the frame, in cursive silhouette, on an elliptical canvas). For a while she made sculpture or big cut-out figures, some of which were kinetic and had moving parts, although she admits that "all I wanted to do was put paint on them." Toward the end of this period, she consolidated her interest in writing, painting, and sculpture into books with small slab-like pages, heavily painted or embroidered. She also made a newspaper for which she wrote and illustrated all the stories and which, to friends' chagrin, she named "The Monthly."

A comparison between the earliest and one of the most recent paintings used to illustrate this essay indicates how near to and yet how far from finding herself Murray was during these years. *Poverty,* from 1964, the year she received her MFA from Mills College, has the basic ingredients of many recent Murrays, especially the 1985 *Not Goodbye.* In both paintings we see a figure and furniture in a room with a door or window and we come in on the action mid-way. In *Not Goodbye,* a woman merging with a table

is being sucked through a yellow doorway at the top corner of an approximately diamond-shaped canvas. In the earlier work, there's a man whose legs extend below the canvas edge on one side of a yellow door and, on the other, the head and shoulders, also in relief, of a policeman—here cast as the wolf at the door. The policeman raps on the door and the inhabitant of the room "hears" his knock via a cartoonish line of dots, dashes, and gray puffs (like Indian smoke signals) which wafts anxiously across the painting. Precursor of various clouds, smoke trails, and other signs of action in Murray's recent work, including the little wavy lines emitted by the woman's topknot in *Not Goodbye*, this line of marks is the only part of the image that moves. In contrast, everything in *Not Goodbye* is in motion: three of the six legs of the woman-table boom out at us, extended into real space by appended canvases; the other three legs are small and fading—like the woman's quite tiny head—as everything is pulled toward the vertiginous vanishing point of the yellow opening. We first experience this movement visually and viscerally. Then, helped along by a title which pleads for things to stay put, we start to decipher its profoundly anxious-making significance, a giddiness of forms in space which is about loss, separation, and maybe death.

When Murray moved to New York in the fall of 1967, she was fulfilling a goal she had had in mind ever since two short visits to the city during her undergraduate years. Her one friend in town was Jennifer Bartlett, whom she had gotten to know at Mills, and Bartlett soon introduced Murray to the artists Jenny Snider and Joel Shapiro, then Snider's brother-in-law. Murray remembers the three of them as "the first

people my own age who accepted me as an artist." During the first few months in New York, Murray saw work that she felt both connected to and competitive with, particularly Richard Serra's process pieces, Keith Sonnier's "eccentric abstraction" sculptures, and Brice Marden's monochrome panel paintings. The whole panoply of Minimal and Process art was "shocking for me. What I felt more than anything else was this kind of rebellion. The mood was that painting was out, that hip people, people who were avant, weren't involved with painting. That was unnerving, but then I didn't give a damn....For the first time in my life I was exactly where I wanted to be."

Happy as she was to be there, Murray continued to resist New York in new work, and this resistance reached its zenith, and final spasm, in a series that took the Empire State Building as its subject. Despite the homage paid the city, Murray displaced its premier (and most phallic) icon into situations that are alternately regional and feminine, in the most clichéd ways.

This is especially true of the diminutive painted plaster casts of the building, framed by stars, lightning rods, and the word "souvenir," and displayed on satin or patchwork pillows. Among the paintings on canvas were *Empire in the Country, Empire with Geese,* and *Night Empire* (the only one surviving), images which transport the building to rural settings and surround it with wildlife, starry nights, rolling hills and innocent little steam engines. The smooth, fastidious surface and tight rendering of these paintings seem completely alien to Murray's usual robust physicality. Still, *Night Empire,* at least, is full of covert signs of things to come. The palette of deep, satisfying colors from all sectors of the spectrum is completely familiar. The train's smoke trails, the yellow beams of light, and the red zig-zags of lightning shooting out from the Empire's upper reaches all play major roles in Murray's work of the 1980s. Even the most obnoxious aspect, the trompe l'oeil border of rippling fabric around the painting's edge—which is maniacally decorated with countless images of Dick Tracy and Little Orphan Annie astride a cross-eyed elephant—has lately been literalized in the ups and downs, and ins and outs, of some of Murray's stretcher

bars. But most of all, the building itself, framed in an aura of glowing blue and red, is an animated inanimate object, ancestor of Murray's equally vital cups, saucers, tables, chairs, and goblets.

Taken together, *Poverty* and *Night Empire* suggest that Murray could have become a rambunctious, not terribly original "regional" artist had not her ambition brought her to New York. There, she had to reconcile, not abandon, her proclivity for animation, narrative, and visual funkiness with the latest strategies of her own generation, the traditions of the New York School, and also the legacy of twentieth-century art in general. It would not happen overnight. It took Murray several years to translate her dramas into original formal terms. But slowly she learned to get the event out of the story line and into the interactions of shapes and space; to condense her love of writing into wonderfully cryptic titles—sometimes poetic, sometimes conversational—capable of detonating a much more profound story line in the viewer's head; and to soothe the frazzled, hysterical tightness of the "Empire" paintings, making a slow-motion, stopped-in-time hysteria one of the true subjects of her art.

The turning point came for Murray in 1971 when she decided she was tired of feeling "so out of it" and wanted her work to be "more affecting"—that is to participate more in the ongoing dialogue between artworks that constitutes the most enduring aspect on any art scene. Help came in the form of bluntly critical studio visits from both Shapiro and Bartlett. Murray remembers that Bartlett in particular "really gave it to me. She said, 'You can do better than this.'" After that, Murray abandoned three-dimensional work completely and went

Poverty
1964. Mixed media on canvas, 84 × 102″.
Work destroyed

out and bought a lot of oil paints for the first time in several years. Changing from acrylic back to oils regrounded her painting and slowed her down, ending the desperate speed with which she had been moving from one idea to another. "The minute I got back into the physicality, I knew I would make some big changes....Subject matter became less important, paint more important."

From 1971 until 1976, Murray progressively took hold of the physical facts of painting. First, line and mark, surface and color were investigated with a directness that she had not allowed herself since the Art Institute and, perhaps due to the return to oil paints, her consciousness of painting's history began to show itself in the work for the first time, providing a counterweight to her love affair with cartooning. It also is here that a feminist aspect of Murray's sensibility starts to manifest itself in a series of subtle re-uses and misuses of images from other art, and we start to see "feminine" versions of the modern masters. Of her increasing penchant for a form of quotation, Murray has said, "Everything's been done a million times. Sometimes you use something and it's yours; another time you do it and it's still theirs."

Three works in particular stand out from this highly transitional period. The one surviving "Beer Glass" painting of 1971 is a reprise of Gris: a jaunty goblet on a surface that is an engrossing bevy of minor adjustments, inexplicable protuberances, and openings—all made with an ease that remains unmatched for several years to come.

In an untitled painting which borrows two of the figures from Cézanne's *Cardplayers,* Murray signals her ongoing emphasis on the unstoppable mutability of shapes and signs. The figures' heads and shoulders, reduced to linear motifs in the "image" at the canvas's center, mutate still more in the surrounding patterned "frame," becoming schematic setting suns, arrowheads, and pine-tree shapes which suggest Indian hieroglyphs. And the colors, although sparsely applied, are right out of *Night Empire,* with the stretcher edge painted bright yellow.

In the 1972 painting *Madame Cézanne in Rocking Chair,* Murray diagrams the banal domestic side of a classic art set-up. Using the Minimalist grid and stick-figures to establish a narrative sequence much like a filmmaker's story board, Murray shows Madame Cézanne sitting for her portrait. Gradually the subject of the artist dozes off and tumbles out of the chair, gets up and reseats herself. This painting also spells out frame by frame the animated, narrative-infused formal relationships that have preoccupied Murray for the last decade, as well as the strange forces activating them. As in Murray's recent work, we see a semi-abstracted figure and a piece of furniture, and both are on the move, changing in shape, size and proximity, as do the elements of the room they occupy. The mysterious force behind all this action is a moonbeam of little dabs of yellow paint. It too changes shape and angle, as it pulls the figure and chair all around and finally out through the door, like the moon pulling the tide. As in *Night Empire,* and more recent paintings like *Beam, Fly By,* and *Deeper Than D.,* Murray's light does not just provide gentle atmosphere, it is a powerful physical force which has a palpable effect on things.

Late in 1972, after working all summer on paintings in which two or three colors were loosely scumbled together into variegated monochrome surfaces, Murray finally was able to relieve her lines of the cartoon-like narrative function they performed so adroitly in the "Madame Cézanne" paintings. That fall she began working on paintings that constitute her first original work: a series of strange linear structures embedded in surfaces which seem to be unusually messy, active versions of Brice Marden's monochrome grounds. A great admirer of Marden's work, Murray remembers wanting to make his surfaces "gushier, gutsier"

Night Empire
1969. Acrylic on canvas, 51½ × 48½".
Collection Susan Murray

and his colors brighter. But for all her new abstractness, there was no consideration of giving up the image, or at least the sign.

Signs abound in these dense little paintings: idiosyncratic grids, ladder structures, circles which almost become faces, a Möbius band, and semi-legible letters. They often suggest bigger, more irrational versions of the mutating hieroglyphs surrounding the "cardplayers" image and, together with the slightly agitated surfaces, they exude an inchoate neediness which is a far cry from the self-sufficient dignity of Minimal art. Although she now often finds these canvases "too cute and quirky," Murray also remembers that "all those paintings are so *made*; the paint really builds them." She also liked (and still likes) "the idea of making a painting that had an 'inside,'" and realized that there had to be "something that was going on inside the paintings for them to really happen for me."

Murray does seem to have been involved in a process of internalizing or submerging the ideas in her work—both emotionally and physically—as a way of making them more abstract, more felt, and more original. The apparent feminism of her sewn paintings and pillowed plaster plaques comes out more organically—and ironically—in a series of rough little paintings with off-kilter triangles scratched into their surfaces all titled *Giant Maiden*. Her usual animation is reduced to a quiet vibration, most clearly in a series of paintings where schematized fan images are titled either *Pulse* or *Heartbeat*. In them, repeating lines, moving across the paintings' surfaces, attempt to measure the very life of the body.

The line paintings culminate in the lushly green *Wave Painting* of 1973 in which the lines break free, multiply and swerve all over the place. The entire surface seems generated by one of Murray's quirky alphabet doodles—a quasi "H" or "J" in the upper left corner—and the result is rather like a Stella "Black Painting" or an Agnes Martin grid run amok. It is animated, totally, if subtly, in motion; its central portion outlines a flattened version of the phantasmagoric genie-shape of later paintings; and it is the great painting of Murray's early years.

Following Murray into the second half of the 1970s, we can appreciate the benefits of her singular process of internalization and reiteration, her restless drive to make an image her own, rather than leave it "still theirs." There's an exhilarating formal drama played out in these years, as well as a great deal of awkward effort, but what's most exciting is the organic way that formal shifts lead Murray to new and deeper meanings or give her new ways to communicate the old ones she'd been so obsessed with during the 1960s. Mainly Murray examined the shape—and its history—like a raccoon with a prized egg. She studied it from every possible angle, turning it over and over, knocking it against things until it finally cracked open and its insides came pouring out.

Inevitably feeling and form went hand in hand. In 1974, a desire for stronger colors and a more emotional impact forced Murray onto larger canvases. In such paintings as *Flamingo,* she diagonally split Marden's monochrome into two triangles of opposing hues, keeping them "taut and flat," as was still her goal, through sheer surface density and by pinning them down with a line or a few dot-sized circles and squares. Of even greater significance is *Middleground,* from the following year, in which Murray seems to have simply pried apart *Flamingo*'s two triangles of color to discover a big autonomous pod shape behind them. In doing this, she found that things didn't have to be pinned down, but could move back and forth in space; also, a kind of animate "being" could be implied without being described.

In 1976 Murray began pushing things out of shape in the literal sense in a series of irregular polygon canvases given a scaled-up Neo-Constructivist treatment, which she ultimately found too purely formal. Much more important among the 1976 canvases is *Beginner,* in which

Beer Glass
1970–71. Oil on canvas, 16 × 14″.
Collection Jennifer Bartlett

Murray in essence begins again. She takes Arp's and Miro's biomorphism under consideration and lets her old interest in cartoon-like animation start edging back into her art. At the time the largest painting she had ever made, *Beginner* is dominated by a big floating bubble pinched in on one side and coming to a sharp beak-like point on the other. Murray calls this form a "big Tweety Bird shape." It is the first of her abstract forms to be a true protagonist, to have an "inside." Looking at it and then looking back, it seems that the excess of personality, so rampant in Murray's '60s work, finally has come to rest in a place where it can be itself, and also be powerfully abstract and evocative.

Beginner brings a stasis and emotional deepening, an increased mysteriousness to Murray's work. With it, Murray announces her intent to grapple with the scale and encompassing power of New York School painting on her own terms—which are adamantly intimate and which nearly always involve the suggestion of something small rendered large, or seen close up. The large shape, with its coiled umbilical cord, is, of course, like a big weightless embryo. *Beginner* is perhaps a late twentieth-century reprise of Miro's *Birth of the World.*

In the paintings of the late '70s, the single shape cavorts with more or less personality, as in *Writer, Spring Point* or *New York Dawn.* Intimations of mitosis are visible in the delightfully Deco double-register genie of *Parting and Together.* The break becomes definite in *Join* and irreparable in *Breaking,* where the nearly hidden image of a parti-color goblet is cracked by lightning such as hasn't been seen since *Night Empire.* Mitosis is complete in *Heart and Mind,* where the geometric and the organic furtively touch from separate canvases. And the separate genie shapes are differentiated into semi-recognizable protagonists in *Brush's Shadow,* becoming alternately a hand reaching for a paintbrush or a fat turquoise Gumby mounting a green rocket ship. In *Painters' Progress* the shapes metamorphose into an artist's palette and brushes and the canvas itself is shattered into nineteen jagged puzzle-like pieces.

Murray's masterpiece of this period is *Children Meeting* of 1978, in which a little wriggling green shape is pinioned by a pink zig-zag which passes through it three times while boomeranging around the surface. Still, the green strains to get close to a big sedate purple shape which is similar to *Beginner's* "Tweety Bird." Here, different parts of the painting move at different speeds and some don't move at all— each element exhibits a different personality or psychology and stimulates a different feeling.

By the standards of Murray's 1980s paintings, most of the works mentioned above, excepting *Beginner, Children Meeting* and the Miroesque *Spring Point,* can seem a bit fragmentary and unresolved, even though each of them tries out ideas that will be put to better uses later. It is not really until 1981 or '82 that Murray gains complete control of the complex means and possibilities of her work. It seems as if she could no longer resist the rather explicit meanings she found pouring out of her shapes as she painted them. When she gave in, the paintings gained a formal and emotional completeness they had previously achieved only intermittently.

Murray first let things get explicit in a slyly self-reflexive way in *Brush's Shadow, Painters' Progress,* and *Art Part;* the artist's tools and hands are allowed into the picture. Then, in *Yikes* and *Just in Time,* another occupant of the studio—the ubiquitous coffee cup—enters the fray, bringing with it the aroma of domestic situations. When Murray takes her imagery out of the studio and into the kitchen and the living room—where it had often been during the 1960s—her art comes most truly into its own.

Like many of her '70s and '80s contemporaries, Murray has taken the formal and literal consciousness that started with Cubism and ended with Minimalism and put it to the service of a

Untitled
1970. Oil on canvas, 20¼ × 30".
Collection Jenny Snider

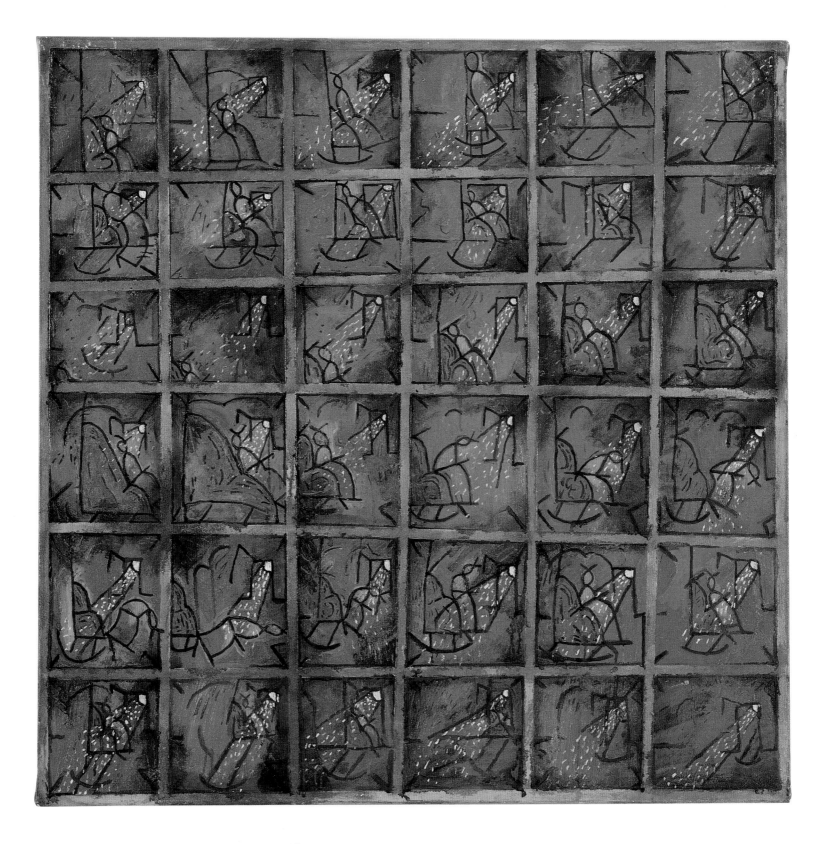

relatively "literary" subject matter, which in her case has the psychological slant and dream-like aspect of much of Surrealism. Her recent still lifes seem especially indebted to Gris in the use of interlocking forms, heavily shadowed colors, and semi-translucent glazing. But Murray's paintings aren't composed of the straight-edged shards of color found in most of Gris' work. Murray is at her best when straight edges are mitigated by curves, by looping arcs or sinuous, undulating ribbons of color, when her Cubist still-life forms have a floating quality reminiscent of Picasso's '30s Surrealist phase. This is very appealing: a woman using Picasso's '30s inflations of the female form in a way that is gender-free, to reanimate the Cubist still life.

Murray's '80s paintings are dominated by the constant threat of unexpected occurrences, of chaos breaking up order, of coffee cups spilling their guts, of emotions erupting, and meanings shifting. As we look at them, these paintings seem to pass through a series of altering states. They change and change us as they go. The contents of Murray's cups and goblets swirl out at us. They are big exclamatory splats which also are hands or crude figural presences or dark rushing ghosts. These changing shapes and events reiterate in visual terms the process of becoming conscious, of coming to see and understand the facts not just of form, but of life itself. And the facts of both form and life are that both are incessantly suggestive and interpretable. What seems at first frightening may become less so, what seems benign and silly may upon examination signal a pivotal, terrifying experience. Thus, the clumsy embrace of table and figure in *Not Goodbye* can suddenly crystallize for the viewer as an attempt to fend off death. Thus, the liquid that swoops wildly out of the lurching cup in *Mouse Cup* also forms a pneumatic six-fingered hand, rather like a rubber glove. As it spills, it curves around, reaching for the cup's handle in an attempt to simultaneously stop the forward spin, flatten the painting to the wall, and restore order. The mutability and continual flux of forms and meanings in Murray's work teach us to tolerate more than one interpretation, to expect additional layers of meaning and feeling behind the

initial ones. In this, Murray's work retraces the process of psychological growth, the incessant retracing of the path between childhood and adulthood that we simplistically call maturity, and in many ways the very procedures of psychoanalysis itself.

And, of course, this fluidity, this tolerance of multiple possibilities, is carried out first and foremost on the formal level. Building her work via a series of subtly fused opposites, Murray refuses to exclude any possibility. She combines geometric and biomorphic shapes; hard edge with feathery, gestural brushwork, with accidental drips and drabs; representation with abstraction; tragedy with comedy. Obtrusive literal shapes, sometimes actively protruding, coexist with, in fact enhance, vertiginous spatial illusions. Murray continually tests and toys with the allusive power of her work by never letting us forget that we are looking at a hand-built, handpainted object. Her images often give out around the edges in order to establish their thinness, their paintedness. Lately, in *Crack-Up* and *Chain Gang*, not only do we see raw canvas, but the stretcher edges themselves are increasingly turned forward, so they also enter into the picture, complete with staples and frayed fabric.

In general, working with multiple shaped canvases has given Murray another set of devices by which to get more "action" into her paintings. In the curved shaped canvases such as *Table Turning, Mouse Cup, Just in Time* and *Yikes,* Murray is able to frame relatively complex painted events in a simple outline, a kind of energetic doodle akin to both her early line paintings and recent drawings. Especially in *Just in Time* and *Yikes,* these outlines also underscore the action by defining jagged

Madame Cézanne in Rocking Chair
1972. Oil on canvas, 35½ × 35½".
Collection Patterson Sims

breaks in the crockery. In paintings using several straight-edged polygonal canvases such as *Keyhole, Beam, More Than You Know* and *Her Story,* the conglomerate shapes actively distort the painted shapes, amplifying even more our sense of disaster and anxiety. In *Beam,* the overlapping canvases, which seem to be cascading off the wall anyway, may actually have caused the beam of light to bend and hit the falling goblet. In *More Than You Know,* the literalness of the table, constructed of five separate canvases, helps turn it into a frightened figure, arms thrown up in panic, a gesture which underscores the outcry of the face at its center and draws our attention to the nearby letter, probably the source of all the turmoil. The split of other canvases behind the table also splits the chair, making it wobble and float disturbingly, creating the sensation of seeing double. In *Her Story,* where a hard-to-see blue woman holds forth from a green chair with a big purple cup raised in one hand, the canvases are punctuated by "giant maiden" triangles. A closer look reveals that each of the three gerrymandered shapes is a big letter: A-A-E...a cry of despair.

Lately, fine tuning and reconsidering things as always, and perhaps worried that her multiple canvases were becoming too much of a gimmick, Murray has returned to more or less single, rectangular surfaces, but even these, like everything else in her art, are subject to multiple pressures. Her most recent canvas shapes frequently suggest open books (harking back to her early writing and book-making days), or a thin sheet or handkerchief draped across the wall, a corner twisted here or folded over there. Sometimes these events interfere with the image, sometimes the image just passes through, from one surface to another. This happens in *Crack-Up* where the edges ripple up and down and two opposite corners fold over, as if the canvas were infinitely malleable—despite its obvious corpulence. In the somberly resonant *Chain Gang,* the canvas is draped on the wall like a piece of drying laundry, and the table, which is its central image, droops accordingly, flapping slightly in the wind.

As Murray puts more and more into her art,

primary devices are frequently downgraded to secondary status, to make room for new developments. In *Deeper Than D.,* the two shapes that come together to accommodate the image—a weightless semi-translucent chair levitated above a room by a beam of light entering through a far-off window—are descended from the "Tweety Bird shape" of *Beginner.* Furthermore, in tandem, they also reiterate the palette shapes of *Painters' Progress* and Murray's other "in the studio" paintings and they're much more effective here, playing second fiddle. In a recent work, *Crack-Up,* the fragmentation of the canvas, so prominent in *Painters' Progress,* is recapitulated on solid ground, where it is actually much more wrenching. The item being torn asunder by conflicting forces is alternately a painting, a table, a person. And in *Not Goodbye,* the paintbrush from various "in the studio" paintings reappears as the figure's topknotted head.

In recycling the art of the past, simple appropriations, or discordant juxtapositions, are not Murray's way. A much more subtle collaging prevails, especially lately. Behind her own rather indelible, ostensibly American, style, we receive continual messages from other images, other times. The yawning bloop of a dog beneath the table in *Sleep,* Murray's only conventionally rectangular canvas in several years, was inspired by the dog in Picasso's *Three Musicians.* In *Kitchen Painting,* a long tube-like figure sitting on a high narrow throne of a chair is reminiscent of Giacometti's and some of Miro's sculpture and an Egyptian queen, but its head is a bit like Mickey Mouse and its long stringy arms encircle a cloud-like splat which bounds off the canvas, thanks to ladle-shaped canvases added to the surface. Is this a cooking

Wave Painting
1973. Oil on canvas, 58 × 58″.
Private Collection

disaster, or a child's disembodied cry for comfort? The face in *More Than You Know* is from Munch's *The Scream* and the exclamatory table, which accommodates a figural reading so easily, can at other times remind me of a horse as terrified as the one in *Guernica,* here galloping out of the picture. The figure who leaves us behind in *Not Goodbye* is a cross between Olive Oyl and Giacometti's *Woman with Her Throat Cut.* But these associations are afterthoughts, ghosts hidden in Murray's art which float up to us slowly.

The degree of ambition, perseverance and concentration which enabled Murray to so completely transform her art is extraordinary, giving ample proof of her belief that "It's not whether an idea is good or bad, it's how far you're willing to go." It is rare to see an artist make such seemingly conventional and at times bad ideas turn out so well, and this fierce coal-into-diamonds distillation also tells us much about women's art in general. It may be that a great deal of ordinary thinking and art-making had to be worked through before something authentic, strong, and diversified started to emerge in quantity, as it has in the 1980s.

To an unusual extent many of the conflicts and antagonisms of art since 1970 are played out in Murray's work. Especially visible are the tensions between the New York hegemony and the American hinterland, between the American concern for newness and the European acceptance of tradition as an essential part of art's progress, and between the broad appeal and instantaneous legibility of popular culture and hermetic high painting culture, implicitly abstract, formalist, and self-referential. Murray's achievement is not that "her" side won in these various conflicts, but that, conflict by conflict, she refused to relinquish her involvement with either side, making them work together without obliterating their differences.

As a painter, she has succeeded in a territory dominated largely by men and masculine subjects. She has put the vocabulary of twentieth-century abstraction to new and different uses, tracing in irresistible formal terms a psychological narrative that is not explicitly feminine but that women, thanks to society's relentless conditioning, know best and most completely. Yet she has made this narrative available and pertinent to everyone by emphasizing that we all start out the same.

In her own indelibly abstract way, Murray has delineated the home front, the domestic situation as the psychological war zone that it truly is, a place of incessant emotional events that are mysterious and open to interpretation. Many artists who emerged in the early 1970s resorted to child-like ploys in order to both absorb and circumvent the dicta of Minimalism. These ploys ranged from Vito Acconci's psycho-regressions, to Joel Shapiro's little house shapes, to Jennifer Bartlett's, William Wegman's, and Neil Jenney's use of primitive drawing and painting styles, even to Mel Bochner's ostensibly modest but intellectually intimidating games with pebbles, matches, and pennies. Murray's early paintings have their own child-like crudeness: obsessive surfaces, awkward lines; they are not concerned with mastery. But Murray is one of the few artists who, as her mastery has increased, has retained as her subject the psychological feel of childhood, the irrational fears of separation, loss and abandonment that most people carry with them into the ranks of adulthood. In a sense Murray's work is part of the still-life tradition that reaches from Gris to Cézanne and back. At the same time, the life in her paintings is anything but still. She pinpoints in rather pure form, those intimate moments when our sense of life's stability leaves us, and everything moves, going away from us and coming toward us at the same time.

Roberta Smith

Not Goodbye
1985. Oil on 5 canvases, 72 × 84 × 14½".
Private Collection

PLATES OF PAINTINGS AND ARTIST'S COMMENTARY

In excerpting the following commentaries from lengthy conversations with Elizabeth Murray, curators Kathy Halbreich and Sue Graze sought to retain the informality and directness of the artist's response to her own work.

Beginner represents a big change in my work. I knew the tight way I had maintained the life of the painting with just color and abstract shape was over. I hadn't done such a large painting in years and I wanted to deal with an organic shape that could be read in a lot of different visual ways. The "Tweety Bird" shape evolved from combining two commas but soon they twisted out to that little pointy place, which is like a parenthesis. I knew the color of it right away. It was the first time I let the paint look so romantic and open by just scraping and brushing it on. I thought of the little mars violet spiral as the voice or the heart or the real inner part of the shape.

Beginner
1976. Oil on canvas, 113 × 114″.
Saatchi Collection, London

Searchin' is about a lunar, oriental mood. I was thinking about a face crossing the moon; only later did I realize how Brancusi-like the face was. I used the pink loop and dark corner to disguise the moon/head configuration. I also wanted the pink line to have an illusionistic feel. I was trying to keep the painting physical and present and I wanted to bring hot, fleshy colors back in; the pink against the bland yellow was like holding my cards to my chest.

Searchin'
1976–77. Oil on canvas, 51½ × 58¼".
Collection Edward R. Downe, Jr.

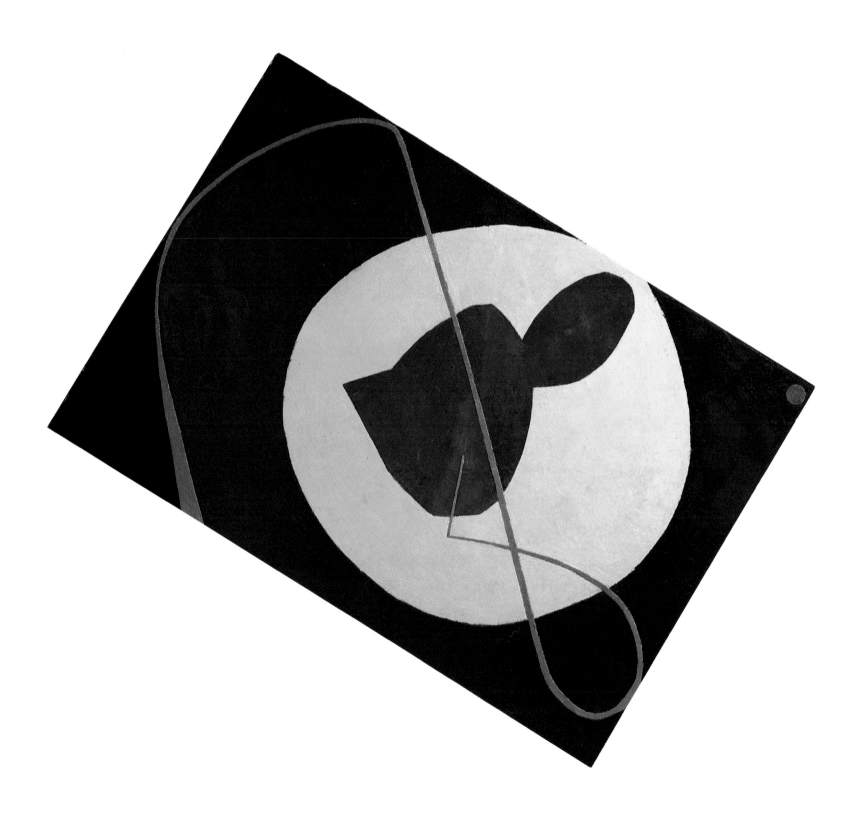

New York Dawn moved away from the constrained, Constructivist look of the earlier work. The exciting parts of painting it were the overlapping blues, the greenish form in the corner, and the purplish black with a white dot which again opened ideas about deep space, about not pulling everything up to the surface or plane. The lines also call attention to the surface. It's a way of saying, "Okay, this spatial play is going on, but this also is just a painting."

New York Dawn
1977. Oil on canvas, 88½ × 65".
Saatchi Collection, London

Spring Point pushes forward a way to use abstract ideas and to begin to turn them into something. I think the dots work like markers and make the painting come alive in certain spots. The blue dot also became the eye of the profile. The yellow dot keeps the space from falling back into nothing.

Spring Point
1977. Oil on canvas, 48 × 41¾".
Collection Susan and Lewis Manilow

Children Meeting, the largest painting since *Beginner,* grew out of a confidence about being able to lay down the colors and put in the goofy shapes that were beginning to emerge. It was exciting to have the green flash into and overlap the purple head/body shape. I'd never allowed myself to use that zany purple; it's a very hard color because it doesn't have a clear emotion for me. It was the last time I was able to use a line moving through shapes as a connector; later it began to feel like a device.

Children Meeting
1978. Oil on canvas, 101 × 127".
Collection Whitney Museum of American Art, New York; Purchase, with funds from the Louis and Bessie Adler Foundation, Inc.; Seymour M. Klein, President.
78.34

Tempest is strongly connected to *Writer*; I did them back to back. *Writer* is the deep, soulful one while *Tempest* is like its title. The colors are astringent yet outgoing, buoyant, exuberant, weird. I was beginning to develop a shape which I pushed a little further with *Writer* where it clearly becomes figurative.

Tempest
1979. Oil on canvas, 120 × 170″.
Collection Memphis Brooks Museum of Art, Memphis,
Tennessee; Gift of Art Today, purchased with matching
funds from the National Endowment for the Arts 80.7

With *Writer,* I was beginning to understand
what the shapes were about and how to get a
picture inside a shape. I also began to understand the conflict of the inner with the outer;
the picture inside the boundary really fascinated me. While I was painting, I decided to
make a figure sitting by a pool. The black and
the pink areas are some kind of land mass. I also
began to see the pink as another profile. I was
thinking about a person writing. It's about soli-
tude and it feels like late, late twilight.

Writer
1979. Oil on canvas, 137 × 74½".
Collection The Saint Louis Art Museum. Funds given
by Mrs. Theodore R. Gamble and the Contemporary
Art Society

When I first developed the two panels of *Join,* it wasn't a formal choice. I was thinking of two profiles touching. The white and the black lines were a joke, I suppose, because it is so blatant to separate something with white and black. But it also is about white and black, those kind of polar thoughts. It was hard to let myself be so outrageously passionate with the color; although the painting conceals a lot, I like that the color belies the grief in the paint. It was a time when I was starting to put things together emotionally. Somebody came in to look at the paintings and said, "Oh, that's a broken heart." It made me cringe for a few seconds; here I am, I'm forty years old and I'm painting broken hearts.

Join
1980. Oil on 2 canvases, 133 × 120″.
Collection Security Pacific Corporation

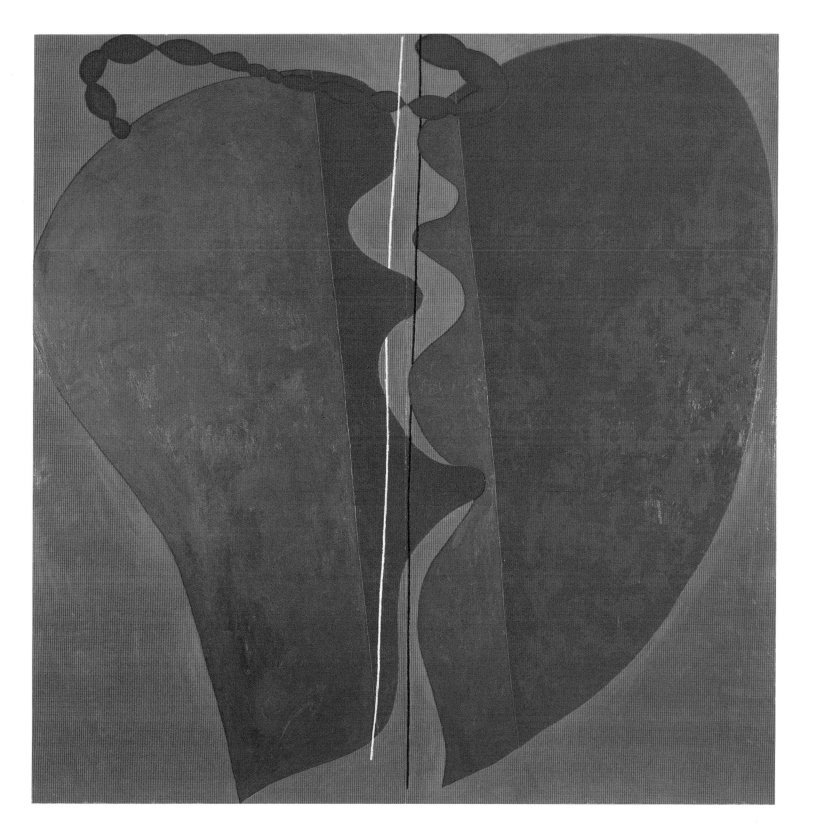

The way *Breaking* happened was that I had four panels. I had done two paintings and was going to do two more, but I didn't really want to. Since I still was interested in those shapes, I put them down on the floor and looked at them together. It was an enormous step because it had never occurred to me to break up or use the shapes together. Immediately a specific image occurred to me: a beer glass. Later, I remembered that little beer glass painting I had done in 1970–71; but here I wanted to pay homage to Synthetic Cubism, which I owe a lot to. Cubism just fits me perfectly; it's like seeing somebody wearing a dress that you easily could jump into. I was starting to think about shattering then and about sculpture again. It occurred to me that the center was absent, that the negative could be the positive. I understood right away that the heart is in the center. The beer glass is breaking in half in an illusionistic as well as in a physical way, and that's the first time I realized that I could do both at once. I was nervous about those yellow lines which are like surprise marks in cartoons. It's like taking a line and using it as a word, which is something that fascinates me.

Breaking
1980. Oil on 2 canvases, 108 × 108″.
Collection Paul and Camille Oliver-Hoffmann

In *Brush's Shadow,* I was thinking of snow men, a figure holding this brush. The blue shape behind the brush animates the painting; in most cases it's the edges of a painting that animate the inner shape. I really modeled the paint here and I felt it was possible to paint all the ways I can paint in one painting. Maybe that's why I think it is a very complicated, goofy picture. I think, too, that the brushes changing into bodies suggest the primacy of art in my life.

Brush's Shadow
1981. Oil on canvas, 116 × 86½".
Collection High Museum of Art, Atlanta, Georgia;
Gift of Frances Floyd Cocke, 1981.54

With *Painters' Progress* I wanted to talk about
the tools of the trade. I was beginning to make
headway and I wanted to turn art back in on
itself. The palette is the head and the brushes
are coming out of the eyehole.

Heart and Mind is a reversal of things, which I really like doing. Again it's the play between illusion and the literal, because in fact the shape becomes the image and the image becomes the shape.

Heart and Mind
1981. Oil on 2 canvases, 111¾ × 114″.
Collection The Museum of Contemporary Art,
Los Angeles: The Barry Lowen Collection

49

I did *Just in Time* the summer that Bob and I fell in love. That's what the title is about. It's the first painting in which I knew I was going to do a cup inside of those shapes. The smoke or steam is very static in this painting which I don't enjoy now, but then I went wild with all the sensual color. The drawing is tight; it's a real still life.

Just in Time
1981. Oil on 2 canvases, 106½ × 97″.
Collection Philadelphia Museum of Art, Purchase:
The Edward and Althea Budd Fund, Adele Haas
Turner and Beatrice Pastorius Turner Fund
and funds contributed by Marion Stroud Swingle and
Lorine E. Vogt

Bean was the first time I attempted to paint pieces of a figure; the white chain is like a skeleton or bones of the brown form. This picture suggests a grammar or different views of the same things.

Bean
1982. Oil on 3 canvases, 117⅛ × 116″.
Collection of the artist

Yikes is my favorite cup painting because it reminds me of a forest. I was thinking of early Cubist landscape painting. It's the color, which I allowed to be strong and saturated, that made me feel like I was inside a forest. Maybe it's a very artificial forest; imagine walking inside one of those Braque landscapes. I also was thinking very specifically about the hand bursting out of the head and a yell created out of the negative parts or the white of the wall. Also, it's the first time I did a canvas which rolls out.

Yikes
1982. Oil on 2 canvases, 116 × 113″.
Collection Douglas S. Cramer

I thought *Long Arm* was about mothers, about parents. It's a cup, but I turn the cup into a reclining figure and the handles become arms. I was thinking of the long arm of the law and then happened to get the Laurie Anderson record where she talks about Mom's long arm. It seemed incredible that the two should connect. I wanted the painting to feel like it had no edges and could go on forever. It is definitely more abstract—the images don't explain the shapes and the shapes don't really explain the image.

Long Arm
1982. Oil on 7 canvases, 107 × 85″.
Collection Martin Sklar

I think *Keyhole* is about finding an image that's a sexual one. That yellow shape is a splash from the cup as well as fingers of a hand. It's the first time I overlapped elements to make that interior shape. I'd just begun to use earth colors and tones; I was thinking about Cubism in terms of color and the relationship of parts. The idea comes from art, not from life, in this painting as well as in *Yikes*.

Keyhole
1982. Oil on 2 canvases, 99½ × 110½″.
Collection Agnes Gund

Beam is another beer glass except there's a real foot coming out of it. The most important part of the painting was going back to the rectangles and letting them come forward like pages of a book, overlapping. I was haunted by a blue window with the beam of light coming out of it. While it's related to the earlier Constructivist ideas, I'd found a way to carry it from one place to another. It was difficult to put the pink triangle in. I kept taking it out and putting it back. There's also the first suggestion of a room by making a horizon line and I said, "Maybe that's floor and maybe that's wall."

Beam
1982. Oil on 4 canvases, 110 × 77".
Private Collection

In *Table Turning* the two shapes are like two people. It's one of the first times I used the table and I felt I had turned the tables on myself in some delightful and surprising way. This also is the first time I allowed for the transparency of paint, and one side of the painting is more physical while the other side is more ghostly. The leg of the table fades through the saucer. There are two time/spaces; it's like daylight and nighttime in the same painting.

Table Turning
1982–83. Oil on 2 canvases, 106¼ × 100½".
Collection of the artist

Sail Baby is about my family. It's about myself
and my brother and my sister and, I think, it's
also about my own three children, even though
Daisy wasn't born yet. It's about childhood and
using yellow.

Sail Baby
1983. Oil on 3 canvases, 126 × 135″.
Collection Walker Art Center, Minneapolis; Walker
Special Purchase Fund

In *Deeper than D.* I was thinking about my mother, who was dying. My mother's name is Dorothy and the D. in the title stands in for her. I was thinking she's really much deeper than I could ever quite comprehend. I don't know why a chair or a room surfaced or why I wanted to enclose these spaces. I really liked having these organic head shapes and putting a room inside of them. The window and the beam of light just felt like a real softness.

Deeper than D.
1983. Oil on 2 canvases, 106 × 102″.
Private Collection

In *More Than You Know* I kept trying to turn the table into a figure and it wouldn't do it. The room just happened; it reminds me of the place where I sat with my mother when she was ill. Once I put the little rectangular shape on top of the green head, it made me think of a book; it was like a trompe l'oeil. I was thinking of Van Gogh, of *memento mori* subject matter, and the paintings by Vermeer of women reading letters which express simultaneously such serenity and anxiety. I wanted to paint the chair very realistically; at the same time, it's like a big heart.

More Than You Know
1983. Oil on 9 canvases, 108 × 111 × 8″.
Collection The Edward R. Broida Trust, Los Angeles

There's a Picasso painting where a dog is underneath the feet of a group. That's the art reference in *Sleep*, but I think the painting is about something trying to get out. I wanted to do an enormous black painting. I returned to the rectangle because I also wanted to see if the shapes were a gimmick, to test their meaning. Afterwards I knew I was bored with the flatness.

Sleep
1983–84. Oil on canvas, 129 × 129″.
Saatchi Collection, London

Can You Hear Me? was the second painting that used the numbers 1 2 3 as shapes for the stretchers; it also includes an exclamation mark with a dot. The painting is about making a sound; I was thinking of Munch, and the green felt painful and screechy. I had trouble sticking to that color so I tried to soften it a little bit with yellow. The formal challenge was to allow the structure of the painting to remain fragmented while making the table and the room out of it. It's just one of those paintings where everything felt necessary once it began to come together.

Can You Hear Me?
1984. Oil on 4 canvases, 106 × 159 × 12″.
Collection Dallas Museum of Art, Foundation for the
Arts Collection, anonymous gift

Her Story is about "now you see it, now you don't." I always come back to turning things into something else. The shapes of the canvases are an E and two As with the E on top. I was going to do A B C, but thought that was too predictable. The dress, the arms, the hands, the head are all made out of triangles; part of the skirt is not there, which makes another triangle where the wall shows through. There's also a cup and chair. There's a pink book in her lap made out of overlaps, a pun I enjoyed.

Her Story
1984. Oil on 3 canvases, 105 × 132″.
Collection Robert K. and Loretta Lifton

Formally or structurally, *Kitchen Painting* is one of the first paintings where I have a shape jutting right out of the canvas. It's a ghost-like painting because of the color, which I haven't been able to do again. I really wanted to do more of a white painting but I couldn't keep it white. The painting again is about family and about being in an interior. A figure is grasping a spoon; I don't know whether the figure is the cook or the eater.

Kitchen Painting
1985. Oil on 2 canvases, 81 × 58 × 14″.
Collection Paula Cooper

Chain Gang is one of those paintings that came together right away, in two weeks. It's about feeding and a kind of darkness; the spoon and the brush are connected. The title comes from the Sam Cooke song "Chain Gang," but I think it's a reference to an artistic imprisonment. Yet the painting was wonderful to do because it's so painterly, almost too beautiful.

Chain Gang
1985–86. Oil on 4 canvases, 114½ × 125½ × 16¼".
Collection Mr. and Mrs. Harry W. Anderson

NOTES ON THE DRAWINGS

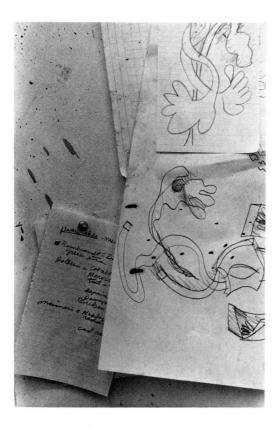

A recent visit to Elizabeth Murray's studio revealed the vitality and diversity of her use of drawing. I saw pastels in various stages of evolution as well as drawings different in character and function. Tacked to one white wall were the paper cut-outs that serve as templates for the manufacture of the increasingly dimensional stretchers of Murray's shaped canvases. A small "idea" sketch, a casually jotted notation, was pinned next to a painting in progress. A comparison of the germinal sketch and the painting suggests the fluidity of Murray's process and imagery: the reaching hand and spoon in the drawing had become a long, blood-red "drip" in the painting. Nearest to the windows, a pastel from the "Open Book" series was in progress, stapled to the wall and surrounded by the ghostly silhouettes of previous drawings. Characteristic of the artist's flexible working methods is the fact that the double-leaved "book" once had been two separate drawings.

Every drawing tends to have its own configuration of sheets tailored to fit the image and, as with her paintings, the format often deviates from the conventional rectangle. The ravelly, hand-torn edges may broadly echo or define the interior forms of the image and, at the same time, contribute to pictorial tensions by confining or abruptly slicing off the swelling, modelled forms held captive within their perimeters. In the case of some of the more intricate and irregular mosaics of overlapping sheets, the slipping, sliding rhythm contributes a tottering instability or centrifugal spin to the image.

When I'm beginning a big drawing, I'll put the sheets of paper up on the wall in big chunks and use a ruler to tear them. I'll eliminate sometimes as I'm drawing or I'll put the paper down on the floor, make the pieces, staple them up, and shift them. Lots of times when I'm shifting them, I'll get

new ideas and I'll tear a little off here or there. It's a pleasure to reorganize the sheets, unlike the paintings which are so finite. Once I get a painting up on the wall, I can shift around the pieces but I can't squeeze it or chop a little bit off as I can with a drawing.

Although Murray tries to keep the time devoted to painting and to drawing separate, the two media always are engaged in an animated dialogue. While, on the one hand, the shaped canvases determined the eccentric contours and collage configurations of the drawings, on the other, the richly worked surfaces of the pastels anticipated the denser texture and greater coloristic complexity of the recent paintings. Although some of the drawings are quite large, they do not rival the scale of the paintings or lose their relationship to the dimensions of the human body.

The energy that goes into a drawing feels much more pointed [than in a painting] because I'm able to hold the charcoal in my hand and get so close to the paper. There's less in the way. It's so easy to just wipe it all down and start over again. It feels like I can think faster and focus more easily with drawings.

At the core of Murray's attitude toward drawing is her requirement that the viewer have a sense of the drawing being made. She allows the image to emerge slowly and to undergo metamorphoses that spring from an instinctual level of consciousness; consequently, most of Murray's drawings present a vivid sense of layering, of changes in direction, of ghostly, half-obliterated traces of previous work. She often scrubs and rescrubs the surface of the paper, taking the sheet to the very limits of its receptivity before acknowledging that the drawing is finished. The visible tracks the artist leaves behind contribute strongly—along with the broad gestural strokes and the overlapping sheets of paper—to the viewer's sense of a drawing in process. Within the modern tradition the drawings of Matisse and Giacometti are perhaps the two most important sources for this interest in retaining a sense of the image evolving layer upon layer or struggling to emerge from a field that has been energetically worked and reworked.

This desire to retain the history of the drawing's evolution is shared by many American artists of Murray's generation as, for example, by her friend Susan Rothenberg. Murray also insists that "ghosts" and layering happen organically and not be self-consciously forced. Erasure, as a positive medium, is so integral to the artist's conception of drawing that it occasionally has been used to define the whole image. (This reminds me of Claes Oldenburg's query as to why eraser was not more often included as a medium when describing drawings.)

Clearly, Murray's choice of pastel represents a strong commitment to richness of surface. The chalks with their velvety bloom are not austere but, rather, inherently sensuous. They also enable her to capture gesture, color, and line in a single stroke. The artist takes advantage of the powderiness of the pastels by either smudging and blending them into smoky tones, continuous and painterly in effect, or making a more precise line that is dry and granular in character. The central "figure" of a drawing frequently emerges from—or sinks into—a scribbled linear ground. The images often are layered and transparent, the overlaid gestural strokes of color being blended by the viewer's eye. Pastels all too often have been used to produce effects of sugary sweetness, but the passages of black charcoal which Murray combines with the pastel colors temper the effect of the overly seductive material and produce more complex, sober color relationships.

Taking up pastel, a medium traditionally associated with the feminine graces and elegancies of eighteenth-century high life, was a nervy act, a clear challenge to the self-conscious purity, sobriety, and intellectuality of geometric abstraction. In Murray's pastel drawings a foundation of abstract thinking—of concern with format, materials and process—does not exclude an increasingly vivid use of life experience. Body language, racy humor, witty references to comic-strip traditions, and visual puns abound.

Clifford S. Ackley

PLATES OF DRAWINGS AND ARTIST'S COMMENTARY

September was one of the first times I set the drawing on its corner; I was starting to think about the shapes and the way the line cuts across the shape. It also was the first colored pastel.

September
1979. Charcoal and pastel on paper, 38¼ × 40¾".
Collection Harrison Augur

In *Drawing for Fall* the past and present come together. The way the line down the middle creates a formal division was familiar, but the snowman shapes and the modeling of the forms were new and have more to do with later work. The drawing has a formality to it yet it's trying to burst out of itself—out of the edges. The color may be too handsome.

Drawing for Fall
1979. Charcoal and pastel on paper, 40 × 25¾".
Collection Jane M. Timken

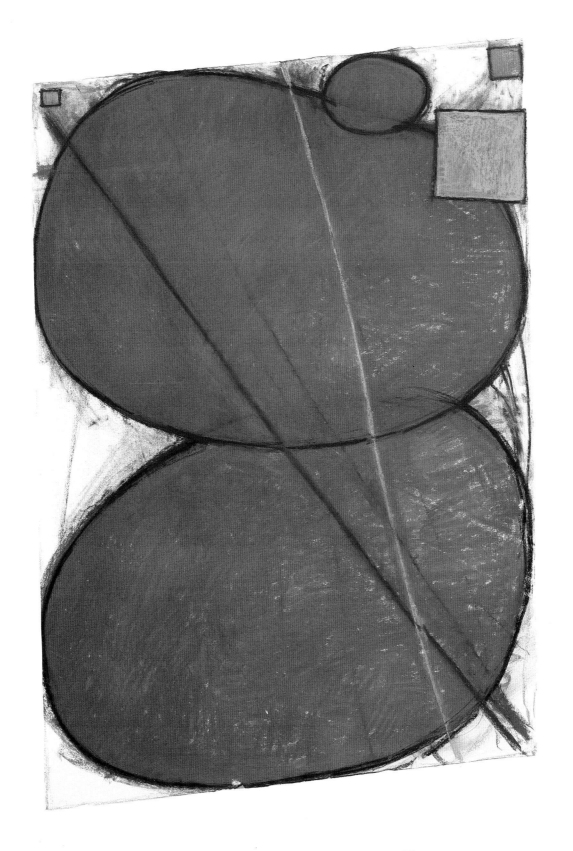

Cup, 1981, was the first drawing that made use of separate pieces of paper. That format felt like an immediate, physical way to get to what I was trying to do with the shattered shapes of the paintings. The infusion of so much color also was something different. I think that happens when you find a new structure—it brings out other innovations.

Cup
1981. Pastel on 3 sheets of paper, 44⅛ × 41⅜".
Collection Barbara and Bruce Berger

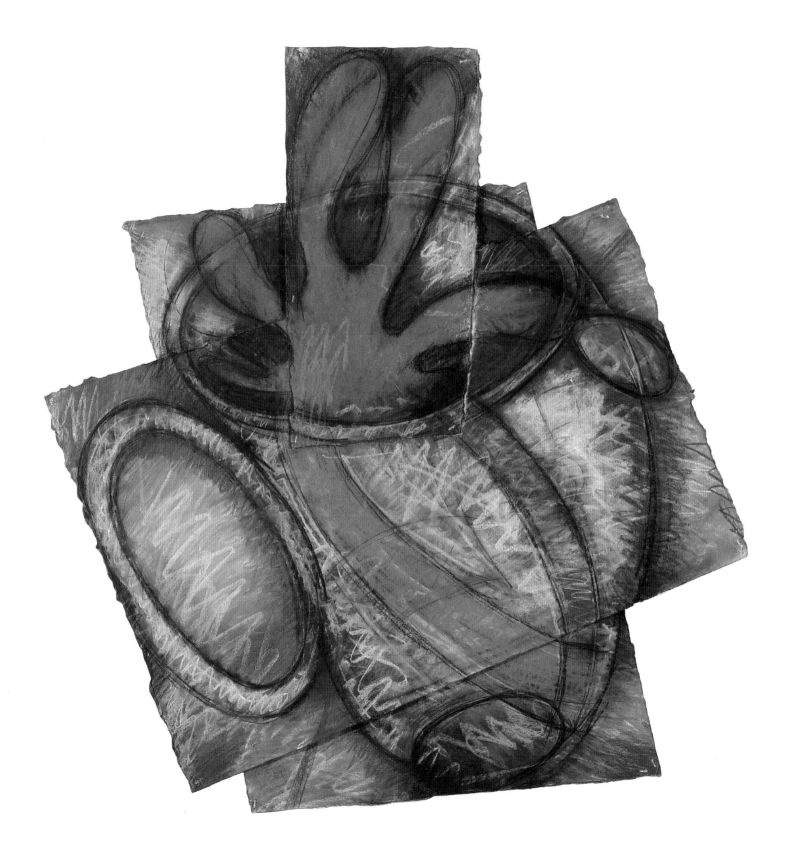

Painter's Partner II was a frightening drawing to do because it was about the painting *Art Part*. It doesn't happen often that there's enough left over in a painting that I want to do it again in a more graphic way. It was exciting to let the hand fade, be ghost-like, next to that evanescent, transparent brush. There's also the strange inversion of the green, painted hand and the pink, fleshy brush. The brush could be a limb, a penis, a baby, or a fish but in my mind it was a brush.

Painter's Partner II
1981. Charcoal and pastel on paper, 52 × 60″.
Speyer Family Collection

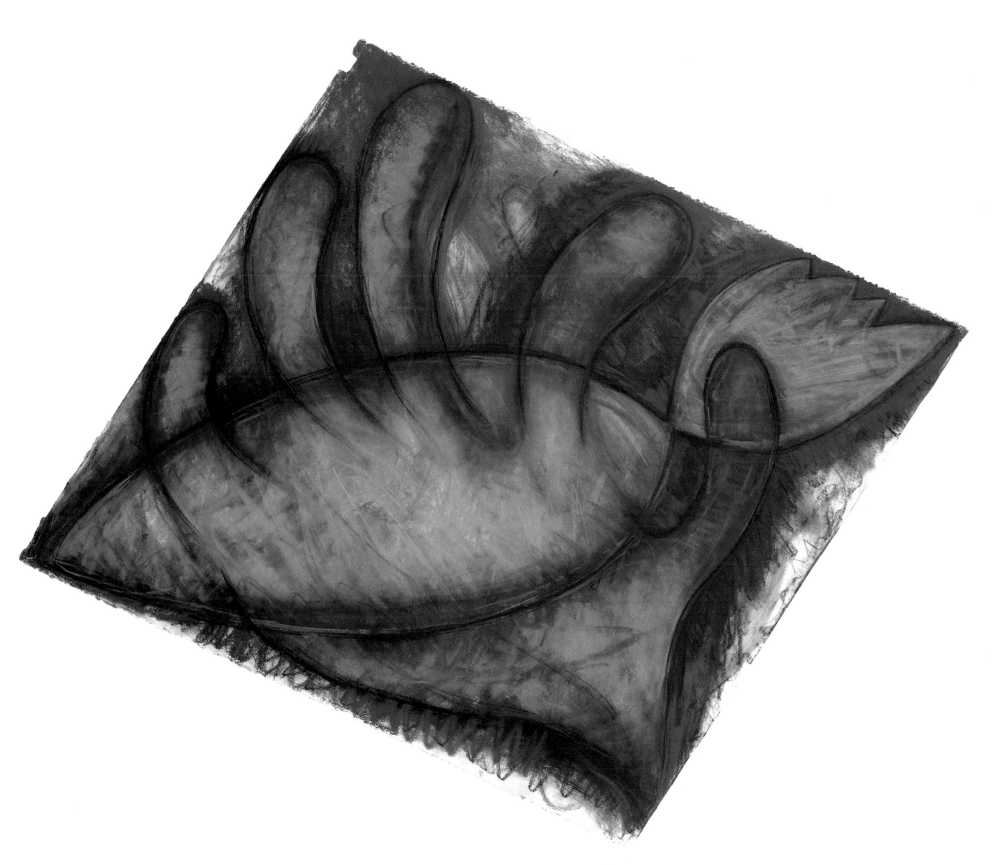

Painter's Partner III is a part of a series. In painting, I don't stop to work out a series, but with drawings I do get to examine things more closely. When I was putting the hand back for the millionth time, I discovered the trace of it and it pleased me. The brush is standing there by itself, almost without the support of a hand, hair blowing in the breeze. I was thinking of *Pilgrim's Progress* and of painters being pilgrims. It is a very romantic activity, like exploring a new shore. It's also intended to be a little bit tongue-in-cheek.

Painter's Partner III
1981. Charcoal and pastel on 2 sheets of paper,
56 × 33″. Collection Marianne and Jonathan Fineberg,
Urbana, Illinois

91

With the *Phone* drawings, I liked the idea of calling out. The phone is yet another image of something ubiquitous that you use everyday and it's the most direct communication. There's no hand in *Phone II,* only the receiver. But by using the dots as eyes and a nose, I suggest a figure. The shadow of earlier shapes creates a kind of energy, a dialogue of form. I started the *Phone II* drawing in Provincetown. I was there for just a couple of weeks and knew I wouldn't finish it, but I like to start a drawing some place other than my studio; I fiddle with it and don't make many choices or decisions until I get back to New York. Then I'll wipe it all down and radically change it. Sometimes I get into a trap because I get so many ideas about a drawing; if I remove it from the place in which I began it, it's easier to see it freshly.

Phone II
1981. Charcoal and pastel on 2 sheets of paper,
40 × 27⅞". Collection Museum of Fine Arts, Boston,
gift of The Charles Z. Offin Art Fund, 1982

This untitled drawing from 1981 is a tumbling figure, but I think you can start from the left side and also see it as a funny comma shape. There's a real pressure against the edge, pushing something into the ground.

Untitled
1981. Charcoal and pastel on 3 sheets of paper,
29½ × 70″. Collection Mr. Andrew J. Ong

Sometimes the cups like *Untitled*, 1981, become a vehicle for exploring a variety of ways of working with charcoal, because they are just great containers. I found the glowing outline which illuminates the cup very exciting to do. It also was funny because it made it this hallowed, luminous object. I guess when I think of cups, I think of morning. I know in the Wallace Stevens poem it figures in the beginning—Sunday morning and here you are sitting with a cup of coffee, watching these swallows fly around. But there also is the drama of the open vestibulé or vessel, which I find compelling. The head/cup, hand/idea comes out of this object. It's really interesting because it's the brain telling the hand how to work out the problem.

Untitled
1981. Charcoal and pastel on 4 sheets of paper,
61¾ × 46″. Collection Paula Cooper

Walk Drawing is a big shoe, and I was thinking of the old nursery rhyme about the old lady who lived in a shoe. I had been looking at the Van Gogh shoes because I thought he had transformed crumby old work shoes into beautiful objects. A shoe has all kinds of connotations. That way, it's like a cup: you don't think about it, but you use it everyday. The idea of a work shoe or a very heavy lady's walking shoe appealed to me. I'm amazed by how the exaggeration of the shoe works; as it twists and turns up, it becomes so many different things—even a figure.

Walk Drawing
1981. Pastel on paper, 35½ × 52". Private Collection

I took both *Popeye* and *Last Night* to the point
where the paper could hardly receive the pastel. In these works, I acknowledged there was a
thing back there I could talk about. It's not just
figure/ground, it's background. The minute you
say background as opposed to ground, you're
talking about narration or something possibly
figurative, illusionistic.

Popeye
1982. Pastel and charcoal on 8 sheets of cut-and-pasted
paper, 76½ × 37¾". Collection The Museum
of Modern Art, New York. Gift of
Abby Aldrich Rockefeller (by exchange)

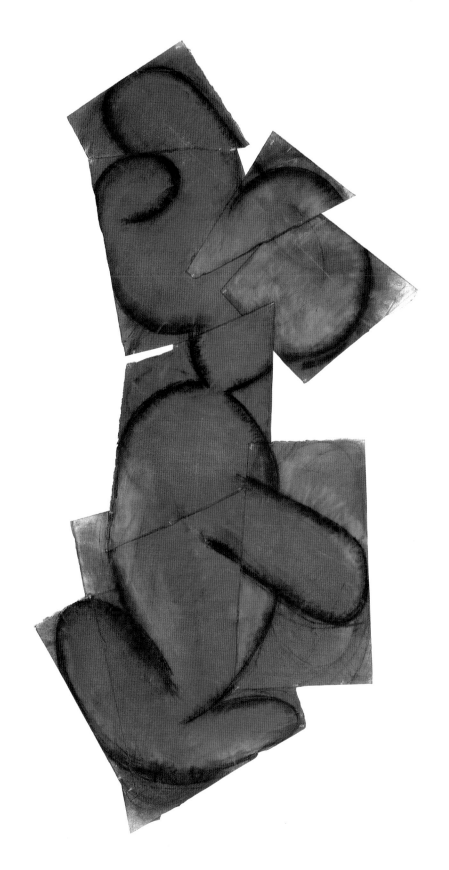

Hear—a big ear—is about the layered feelings surrounding the end of therapy. I was also thinking about my favorite da Vinci drawings of babies inside wombs as I was making the outer layer and then the bean or embryo shape. The drawing is very physical; it's rubbed away and built up again.

Hear
1982. Pastel on 2 sheets of paper, 30½ × 35″.
Collection Robert H. Halff

Last Night is the first time I had an opening in the drawing. In a formal way, it's having negativity inside, of saying, "This is the center, but it's not there." That's psychological need. There's something funny to me about having all that paper and then having nothing. It gets to be a focus or a force that I can work out or off of.

Last Night
1982. Pastel on 8 sheets of paper, 65½ × 52″.
Permanent Collection, Massachusetts Institute of
Technology

I loved doing these tree drawings. They are real simple. *Black Tree* is just a couple of pieces of paper, overlapping. With a couple of these drawings I blackened the paper and then erased out the forms. I wanted to make the lines of trees; it's so wonderful because the trunk could be a neck and the foliage a head with hair or ears. It was a relief, felt refreshing, to deal with black and white. It's like life; occasionally you have to go back to the bare necessities. Here I went back to the bare essentials of art making; one piece of charcoal on a white piece of paper. It clears out my head to limit myself that way.

Black Tree
1982. Pastel on 2 sheets of paper, 48 × 36″.
Collection Estée Lauder Cosmetics

Sophie Last Summer is a drawing of Sophie crawling and crying.

Sophie Last Summer
1983. Charcoal and pastel on 5 sheets of paper,
52⅛ × 26″. Collection of the artist

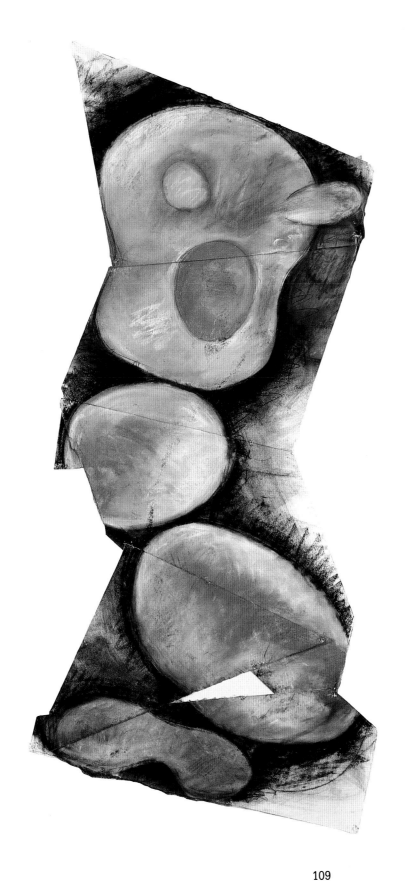

Untitled, 1984, is related to the other shoe drawing. I did enjoy doing that blue.

Untitled
1984. Pastel on 2 sheets of paper, 35 × 24½".
Collection Mathieu Carrière

In *Untitled,* 1984, I went back to the hand grasping something. I put a little piece of eraser inside the palm so it's related to *Painter's Partner* in that they're very much about the tools of the trade. I guess that little bitty thing also could be a fetus: actually Daisy would have been about that size inside of me at that point.

Untitled
1984. Charcoal with rubber eraser on paper, 44 × 30".
Collection Sari and Rick Swig

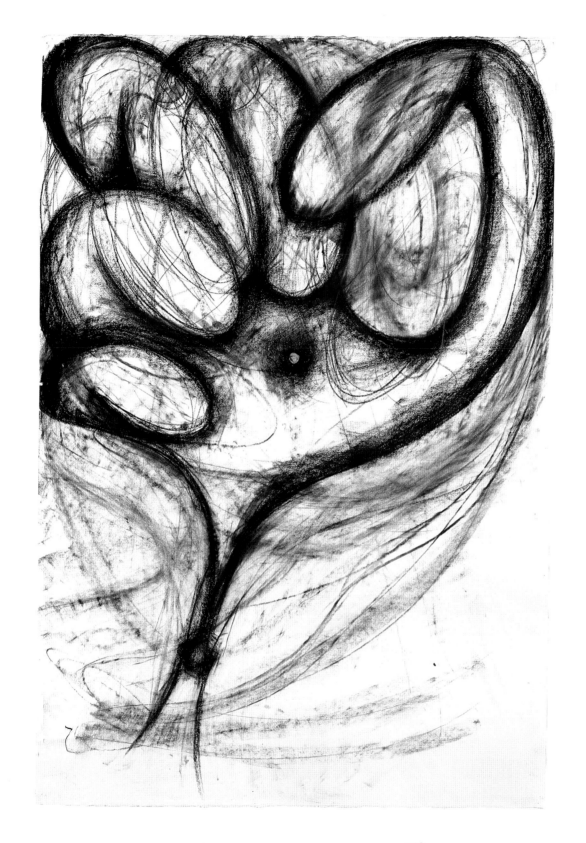

Palm includes a piece of wood in the middle of the hand. It is about a palm and a tree. This drawing puts together the animal and the vegetable, but it lacks a certain kind of craziness. Emotionally, it's just straight up, frontal.

Palm
1984. Charcoal and pastel with wood on 5 sheets of
paper, 59 × 29″. Wellington Management
Company/Thorndike, Doran, Paine & Lewis Collection

In *Both Hands* I was thinking about something very similar to a book opening. The color seems very mysterious, somewhere between organic growth, the soil, and death. It was strange to do because I was gluing those clay pieces on it. It's a bit ghoulish and passive.

Both Hands
1984. Charcoal and pastel with clay on 2 sheets of paper, 17 × 52″. Collection Drs. Steven and Sara Newman

I did two drawings right before Daisy was born about babies, spoons and organs. I think they are very indulgent because they were so much fun to do. I don't think I could do them again unless I was back in that week of time—mucking around in the studio, trying to feel productive, wanting to work.

Untitled
1985. Pastel on 2 sheets of paper, 47 × 52¼".
Collection Robert and Gayle Greenhill

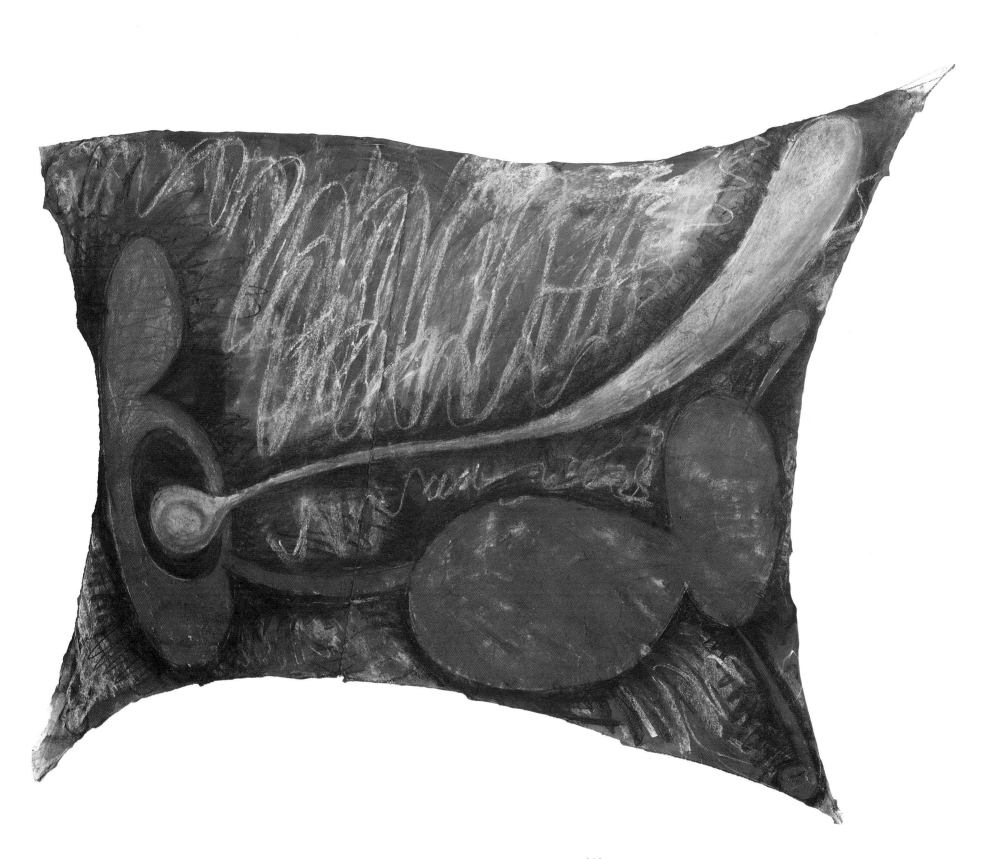

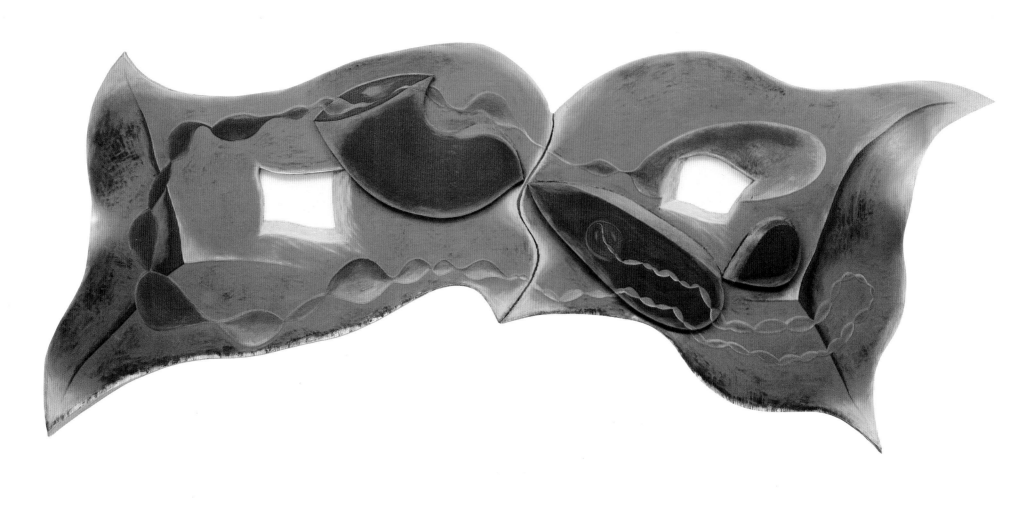

INTERVIEW

Sue Graze and I began this peripatetic interview with Elizabeth Murray in Upstate New York early in the summer of 1985. We gathered first at Murray's cottage which is set in the midst of orderly corn rows surrounded, in the distance, by hills voluptuous both in contour and color. Moving from the kitchen table, we crossed the yard, spotted with the pink of children's balls and newly planted roses, to the barn—a warm weather studio. With chunks of light and swallows falling through holes in the roof, we talked about the beginnings of a painting later titled *Open Book*. A season passed before Elizabeth and I began meeting erratically in her loft in downtown New York to edit transcripts. A home which houses studios for both wife and husband, a poet and performance artist, the loft is filled with paintings and drawings by friends. In the studio, at a makeshift table not far from the sight and sound of Murray's two daughters, we drank coffee from oversized cups; we freely added and subtracted history. Now, a full year's cycle completed, the interview too is done.

KH

INTERVIEWER: One of the obvious places to begin is with childhood. Were there things you remember making as a child?

ELIZABETH MURRAY: I first remember drawing a pipe and an elephant; I remember it so clearly because I knew I had replicated something, like having the idea "elephant" and having it be elephant. I must have been three years old or so. I think the pipe had something to do with my father. I don't know whether I was thinking "pipe" or "elephant" before I started to draw; I was just getting enormous pleasure in drawing the rounded forms of the elephant, the beautiful way its ears, feet, and trunk-like legs go.

The next thing I remember drawing is a profile of my uncle and the adults laughing. It must not have looked like him, but they knew the pleasure I derived from the act itself.

Is there something particularly compelling about a profile?

It can be an abstraction. You can make a line that can be other things besides the silhouette of a face. It's not so descriptive, really.

I've read about a series of drawings called "hand" drawings. Was the hand a stand-in for the whole person?

I must have felt it was, because it was the most important part for me. Although I drew faces, I hardly ever drew full figures.

Can you tell me something about what you called your sex drawings?

I think I started to do them when I was in fifth grade. It was fun sitting around with a bunch of girls and drawing my idea of a sexual act, which was a man, fully clothed in a tuxedo, and a woman, in a negligee with openwork stockings, sitting on a couch. I would sell my friends the drawings for a quarter.

Open Book
1985. Oil on 5 canvases, 98 × 230 × 11″.
Collection Whitney Museum of American Art,
New York.
Gift of the Mnuchin Foundation. 85.74a-b

Threaded through all your work is this constant seesaw between what's sexual and what's romantic, what's revealed and what's covered.

I loved doing those drawings because they were surreptitious. The big thing was to make them as realistic as possible. I drew constantly: my parents, my brother, scenes of cowboys and Indians, tons and tons of men dressed in suits, many stories of detectives in search of something. I was more interested in making action drawings of what men do out in the world than I was in depicting scenes of domesticity. Drawing was something of an escape just as reading was. I was aware that my drawings were different from what other kids were doing, and I was very proud of my skill. It was a way of getting attention; I think that's in the background of everyone who becomes an artist. I know that it must have saved me to have the ability recognized.

Did you always know you were going to be an artist?

I was going to be an artist, and I was going to go to the Art Institute of Chicago. It was that simple. I thought I'd be a commercial artist; all my ideas about art came from looking at comic books. I remember writing to Walt Disney to ask if I could be his secretary; I also sent him a sketchbook. I think cartoon drawing—the simplification, the universality, the diagrammatic quality of the marks, the breakdown of reality, its blatant, symbolic quality—has been an enormous influence on my work.

Can you remember what was pleasurable about comic books?

It wasn't the story; it was color and drawing. I never liked looking at the super-realistic ones, like the romance comics which I did read. I had my favorites—Donald Duck, Little Lulu, Orphan Annie, and Dick Tracy. When I think of Orphan Annie, I think of the brown of the dog, the red of her outfit, and the enormous amount of darkness. In Dick Tracy, there was something very harsh about the drawing. I think it is more abstract than the others; it's very sharp and strange in the angular way it breaks down— almost Egyptian.

There may be a connection between how a comic book is laid out on a page, from box to box, and the sense in your mature work of how one form evolves into another shape. It is explicit in an early painting like *Madame Cézanne in Rocking Chair,* in which you use the comic-strip format.

Well, comic books are like slowed-down film in the way time and sequences are framed. I did a lot of painting using that structure. Of all the art forms, it is film I admire most outside of painting. If I were going to try to do anything else, I would try to make a film—which I'm sure half the artists in the world would tell you. Language and image come together in motion, from one event to another.

Time is an important part of your pictures. There's not only an internal velocity among the parts, but in the shattering. The viewer needs then to reassemble, decode.

I think you receive the painting in its whole shape but slowly piece the thing together. It is important to feel there is an illusion of motion, an illusion of things passing before you. I think it's part of my fascination with the open book or with smoke disappearing—they are things in process. I remember those Disney movies where they opened the book and the story begins.

You've spoken about beginning to understand the power of art through the magic of a Cézanne painting at the Art Institute, the school you entered in 1958.

In retrospect, it's quite an unremarkable painting except for some beautiful *petits fours* which are stacked like tiny logs. But for some reason, that painting was the first in which I lost myself looking. I had seen it almost every morning and every afternoon for a year, but suddenly I really looked at it and understood what art was. It sounds religious, but it is not the same thing as having a revelation. It's very quiet. I just realized I could be a painter if I wanted to try. Before that experience, I thought artists were like Picasso or Michelangelo; they didn't have any reality to me. That understanding came later.

Paul Cézanne. **The Basket of Apples,** c. 1895. Oil on canvas, 24¾″ × 32″. Helen Birch Bartlett Memorial Collection 1926.252. © The Art Institute of Chicago, All Rights Reserved

You mentioned that Cézanne's spirituality impressed you.

His apples are more than apples, the trees more than trees. I don't think of him as an analytic artist. He is passionate in his belief that all things share some common qualities: the rock and the apple are painted the same way, and the boulder is as important as Mont Sainte-Victoire. Everything became ordinary, yet seen singularly; in this way Cézanne might be seen as a precursor to Duchamp. I also just loved the physical quality of his painting—he's such an inventor with paint.

What are those apples?

You can be analytical and say they are spheres, but sometimes they feel like they weigh hundreds of pounds and other times they're as ethereal as feathers. I think his attraction to them was as a way of finding how to go around a form with paint, how to describe something. I think they're just paint containers for him.

Why would he want to contain paint?

To me it makes complete sense. If you are painting a thing, you have a chance to have a boundary—a reference—that's given; then inside that boundary you can make anything happen. Cézanne also tried to make simultaneously a form out of an outside and an inside. His painting around the form was as intense as the paint-

ing of the form; in a sense, there was no figure/ground. When he's painting an apple, he lets you inside through its diaphanous surface. Apples are the heart and soul of the painting. It has to do with finding a way to make something very spiritual through a physical means.

Yet it is a very common fruit.

That really interests me. I also like the calm of the cups, apples and vases on tables. It was very soothing to me because, when I began to paint, there was this rule—maybe it came from Picasso—that you constantly had to invent and then reinvent subject matter. But Cézanne just painted apples again, and again, and again. Each time it was more and more interesting. It seemed a kind of self-acceptance—a sense of the world seen in a dew drop—that appealed to me.

Do you think that there is anything sexual about the apples?

Oh, yes. It's really *the* symbol between the snake and Adam and Eve. Cézanne also painted sculptures of little boys, cupids. Similarly, the portraits of his wife (whom he both had a lot of trouble with and was very attracted to) are rather erotic pictures even if she looks unhappy and a little unwilling, and he paints her with such ambivalence. Those portraits are such tender, exquisite paintings; *Madame Cézanne in a Red Armchair* is just an extraordinary painting.

I'm trying to suggest how a certain loaded iconography relates to the still-life imagery in your work, too.

No one could be more surprised than I to realize that many of my paintings of the last four or five years are really still-life paintings. Cézanne also was obsessed with the paint, with describing this fruit or this vase in just the right way. That is an obsession I can really understand.

But aren't you chasing the cup in the same fashion he followed the apple?

I don't think it is exactly the same. I'm more conscious of wanting the cup to be things other than just cup. Cézanne wasn't pushing that transcendence, but was trying to hold the world steady. I think Cézanne wanted to paint in a classical manner, like Poussin, but he couldn't maintain that control because it wasn't the truth. He had to let the paint slip away from him. I think that struggle drove him nuts.

What do you think of The Bathers?

I know a lot of what I do comes from thinking about them. In one of my favorites you only see the backs of the bathers as they are clunking into the water, with arched trees overhead. The trees are just bigger versions of the figures. What I love about them is the awkwardness of the forms and how they barely become figures. To draw the human body in this clumsy, almost oafish, manner goes right to my heart. All his peers were drawing beautiful figures, but Cézanne says instead, "This is what we are." The Modern's [Museum of Modern Art, New York] picture of the man standing in the pool of water is just a wonderful depiction of the self.

Were there exhibitions you saw as a student in Chicago that were especially memorable?

The Art Institute had two exhibitions that struck me. One was the Beckmann exhibition, the other of Chinese landscapes. It was the first time I noticed how space and scale worked in Oriental art...huge, expansive mountains with small people, all in a very compressed space. Unlike some of my peers, I wasn't interested in the narrative aspects of the scrolls. Nor did I share their fascination with German Expressionism; at that age I was susceptible to the angst and turmoil, but I didn't think the Expressionists were very good painters.

Technically?

I hate to use that word. It's more a feeling for paint; it's as though they really didn't care about it. But Beckmann was an incredible painter, and I made direct copies of his work when I was in school. I also did millions of self-portraits, all heads drawn with black lines. I liked his subject matter which seemed so introspective and searching. He was a painter who used the events of his day almost as symbolic

Willem de Kooning. **Excavation,** 1950. Oil on canvas, 6′ 8⅛″ × 8′ 4⅛″. Logan Purchase Prize. Gift of Mr. Edgar Kaufman, Jr. and Mr. and Mrs. Noah Goldowsky Goodman Fund 1952.1. © The Art Institute of Chicago, All Rights Reserved

themes, and yet he did it in a way that wasn't simply topical or politically illustrative.

When I was getting closer to feeling some of myself in the act of painting, I would run upstairs at the Art Institute to look at de Kooning's *Excavation,* at how he physically moved the paint across the surface and then I would go back down and try to copy that gesture.

There was another show that was more important than anything else. The last year that I was there, the Art Institute had one of their American Annuals. For the first time, I saw a new, huge Pollock, a stroke-y Tworkov, a Rauschenberg, and a Johns. It was the first time I saw New York painting and it really shocked me.

Suddenly art wasn't an historical phenomenon?

Right. It was happening in front of my eyes. It wasn't just copying Matisse and Picasso. It was being invented. I've never been deeply moved by a Pollock, but when I looked at his work, I remember thinking, "If this man can do this and it can work, then everything is totally free."

Did it ever occur to you that you were looking at work made only by men?

It never occurred to me. There was no tradition for a woman to be a painter, although, oddly enough, painting always seemed a feminine pursuit. In America, for instance, since the arts only rarely were considered a masculine profession, I think it's no accident that Pollock and others in the New York School felt compelled to exaggerate their masculinity. All the art I learned from at that time was made by men, but in the end, art transcends gender.

What led you to graduate school?

During the last year at the Art Institute, I was the only woman of a dozen candidates selected for consideration for a big fellowship. You got about $2,000 or $3,000 to go to Europe which, in 1962, was a bundle. When I didn't get the fellowship, I was really crushed; I stayed around for the summer, working on my own for the first time. Some friends of mine were applying to graduate school. I knew Léger and Beckmann had been at Mills College in California so I thought other good teachers might still be there. I applied, and they gave me some funding. I got there in my black leotards and my raccoon make-up and went immediately into culture shock: all those beautiful California girls with beehive hairdos walking around that manicured campus. I was incredibly homesick.

Did it take you long to start working?

No, that was the first thing I did.

Did the work go through a transition?

It really changed a lot because there was a wonderful guy named Carlos Villa, who made immense, beautiful paintings with cheap oil paint. He took me under his wing. In a few months I was heaving and throwing the paint on my own huge canvases. They were cruddy and gooey with all these little amorphous shapes floating around in two or three colors. I started looking at Gorky and de Kooning a lot more. I think the person who got me interested in Gorky was Jennifer Bartlett. She was an undergraduate in a dormitory for which I had been hired—mistakenly—as a second house-mother. I started to read Auden, Yeats, Rimbaud, as in college I had escaped into Burroughs, Joyce, Kafka and Freud and, earlier still, into Willa Cather, Carl Sandburg, and Somerset Maugham. I played the Brandenburg concerti again, again, and again. And Verdi. I started to listen to *Tosca* and the *Requiem*. Lots of Baroque music, which I had never heard before. Finally, I got a teaching assistantship and moved to San Francisco.

Did the landscape or light affect your work?

First of all, I was frightened by it. When you come from the flat Midwest, you don't see too many mountains. I thought it was absolutely gorgeous and scary.

In its expansiveness?

The green of the hills and the motion, the way they moved down into the water. I had never seen an ocean and I was really stunned by the Pacific.

Did it find its way back into the paintings?

I don't know. I could never talk about how I used something directly, but I think everything you see and do affects your work. The awesomeness of the landscape probably had something to do with the increased size of my paintings. But I really think that my art comes from other art, from looking then at Rauschenberg and Clyfford Still.

How do you work with other art?

I don't think I take something and use it directly. When I see something, it comes through me and there is a transference of the information. Even though somebody might not recognize something I'm using, I don't think I've ever used anything from art without being very conscious of it. I may use things from life, like the hand motif you pointed out, but those things are much more subliminal. Sometimes, when I'm stuck on something, I will go get a book of pictures or poems.

You have been liberal in quoting from literature as well as from visual art.

I've read a lot since I was a child; *Gone with the Wind* was a favorite, and for years Scarlett O'Hara represented my ideal of female rebellion. The book *The Second Sex* was important to me when I was in high school. It was the first time I thought about women in the world and understood the emotional, psychological and political differences between the genders. I was fascinated by the idea you were not just created but formed. But there is no direct connection between painting something and thinking about literature.

What artists have been influential?

Everyone always mentions Matisse as an incredible colorist, but I prefer Picasso's palette. Matisse's color is too soft and local for me. Picasso's is harsher, stronger, more abstract. I am just more sympathetic to the emotional range of Picasso. I can think of a lot of paintings that are important to me. There's Rembrandt's last self-portrait in the National Gallery in London. When you walk in, you know that's what art is about; it's this incredible communication of age and depth and sadness.

When you return to look at these paintings, are you looking for that experience or looking at how it's done?

It's learning something even more important than how to paint. It is an affirmation of humanity. For example, Donatello's sculpture of Mary Magdalen expresses such a vivid feeling of the person; you experience an angst which is surprisingly contemporary in tandem with infinite compassion. He's one of my favorite artists.

At one point didn't you stop painting and begin to make sculpture?

Well, it started to happen slowly in San Francisco where I began to glue and nail together paintings. When I started teaching in Buffalo in 1965, I concentrated on Oldenburg who has been a big influence on me. I loved his fan, hamburger, and car. I worked with wood and cloth; I got an old treadle sewing machine and made things like a huge armchair with a figure

in it which I called *Daddy Reading the Newspaper*. I did an enormous pair of pants with huge shoes. I put motors in the knees so they turned around! I made canvas roads and sidewalks.

Do you know why they needed to become more physical or more literal?

I'm not sure, but I've observed from teaching that there's a point when many young painters need to take their work off the wall and realize it three-dimensionally because they can't get everything in there that they want. I can't exactly explain the impulse, but suddenly flat painting isn't satisfying. My works began to get so elaborate I didn't understand how to make them; it probably was fortunate I realized then that all I wanted to do was paint on these structures since they always were more about compression than going out into space. Finally, there's a kind of miracle involved with paint. It's just this stuff in a tube which you squeeze out. It's this physical thing, yet you use it as a transforming agent.

When I try to understand the basic ingredients of painting—the issue of illusion on a flat surface—I can get so lost in that decoding.

That reminds me of another painting that really influenced me. It's Seurat's *La Grande Jatte* because it's like a theater—miraculously you work your way through one scrim at a time, each one created out of dots.

Today the overlapping elements in your own work seem like a muscular set of screens, almost like tissue covering bone. Didn't the sculptural procedures follow you on into paintings such as *Madame Cézanne in Rocking Chair*?

That's not really how I think about it. The shapes are like layers that are twisted or turned around or on top but they can always be compressed again—flat against the wall. I think a lot of those ideas come out of Johns' flag paintings and the eerie painting with the body parts in it. He uses paint as an active kind of layering. He molds it, glues things on, or uses templates until the paint begins to have a concreteness, which reminds me of Cézanne.

Last night I was thinking about the painting I started out in the barn [*Open Book*]. I said to myself, "Every time you start a painting, why do you always feel it has to be better than the last one? It's like one-upping yourself." And I remembered what we said about Cézanne. Every time he made an apple, he thought about it anew. It never became a formula or a mannerism. I was thinking about this today, going, "I know it's going to be another room. But it has to be different. It has to be better. I can't think of anything else to do. Maybe I'll never think of anything else to do." It's not what you paint, but how you're feeling about it and how you're painting it. All you've got is the paint. I think it's a sensual, physical thing—but paint has very different meanings in different hands. I want the physical nature of the paint to be there, but the thought processes are important to me too.

The viewer also approaches the work in a very physical way.

It always is amazing that such a private thing can be communicated. What the paint feels like on the surface of the canvas is such a crucial, elemental expression.

Are there certain feelings or ways of painting you would excise from a picture?

I find anything I want to excise comes back. I just want to include all possible ways of painting. Making art is more about seeking than negating.

So you're giving yourself permission to do anything?

Yes, but it's impossible. You can't do anything you want, but having the fantasy you can is important when you're making a work. I think that tension—the tension of wanting to do it and not being able to do it—is exactly where the art is.

How do the way of painting and the imagery in the painting work together?

One thing comes out of the other. The paint really makes the image; the paint itself discovers the image. It's very similar to looking and finding images in clouds—a game I play a lot.

There are hundreds of either/or propositions in your work, of opposites that come together and break apart...of carved or drawn, balance and wobble, contained and spilled, being and becoming.

I haven't read Kierkegaard for years, but it reminds me of his struggle to be a religious person. Probably because of my Catholic background, the question of God's existence was a big issue in my life. When I decided there was no God, it was an enormous statement to make to myself. Kierkegaard was important to read because his philosophy is based on the idea of acceptance through faith, faith even though the world you're living in makes it impossible to consciously think there could be a God. My work has a lot to do with conflict. Ultimately it is about affirmation, but to get to that point I pit opposites against each other—in terms of color, form and, now, actual physical shapes. It's about posing an impossible proposition and trying to find a way it can work physically. When the painting comes together, it's a knitting of oppositions; that coexistence is where the satisfaction resides. That's the way everything works, like men and women.

Heart and Mind?

All the opposing things you deal with everyday. I don't think everybody feels that as forcefully as I do; I must be trying to balance extremes in my own personality. I began to understand what I was doing with *Painters' Progress* and *Art Part*. They were so psychologically satisfying because I finally realized the meaning of shattering and of putting an image inside the shattered parts that would make them whole again. Many artists don't believe there's a healing potential in working, but I constantly bring up deep difficulties in my character and try to sort them out when I am painting. When I was working on those paintings I kept thinking, "What am I doing? This is such a silly idea. Why am I going on with these shapes; why don't I just go back to painting flat paintings? This is ridiculous." Somehow I put myself into the position of feeling very anxious about an idea and about following my nose. That was a real self-revelation. And for about 24 hours I really felt on top of things.

There are a lot of psychological motifs in both the language and the shapes you have used over time. For example, the title of the drawing *Hold On*.

> The name clearly was intended to allude to the many emotional states of holding on, but it's a joke too. You say to someone on the phone, "Hold on," while you literally are grasping the instrument. That's different from the desperate holding on just before a fall. Or the bittersweet terror of holding on to a person. I love when words can be meaningful to the painting and the painting can be meaningful to the words. The best titles come in the middle of the painting process.

So, there is a relationship between language and image. There are a lot of puns in the paintings.

> That is something I feel about living. There's a great quote of Tennessee Williams'; he says something like, "Somewhere deep under the earth, there is but one book, and it's either a mystery book or a big joke book." It struck me that things go either way. Sometimes things are completely mysterious. Then you realize, "No, it's painfully simple and painfully funny."

It's not accidental, this yoking of various grammars, of images and words. If you look at the shapes, there's a comma, a parenthesis, an exclamation mark.

> That's quite purposeful, although I don't always have a sense of where it's going to lead.

Is there something purposeful about the pause suggested by a comma?

> It's making the stop happen in actual space; it says, "Wait a minute." It's also a shape that becomes. It's a bird-like shape that takes off from a little point. A comma is the most common form of punctuation; it's a connector as well as a stop. I mean, it's not like a period which terminates something. It suggests there's more to come.

The comma is a perfect reflection of the evolutionary cycles that turn up in your work. In one painting the comma becomes a plume of smoke which then becomes a body.

> I guess I've been painting the same things all my life. From the pipe to the elephant. It's working out images that are very meaningful before you know why they are meaningful. Maybe the pipe flattens out and becomes the comma. It's also a very female form, even though it is clearly associated with men. It's a combination.

Which is very pervasive in your work. I'm tempted to shy away from the sexual imagery but I can't.

> Well, it's there, and sometimes it shocks me. I like it. Sometimes I find that things that are frightening are the most interesting.

Is it frightening because it's taboo or because it's potentially feminine and you fear being labeled a woman painter?

> I think it's more because it's revealing. The issue is not indiscretion, but there's a point at which the revealing is not interesting because it can become too self-conscious or arch. It's not innocent. Writers such as Bernadette Mayer and Eileen Myles write about their sexuality in an artful way. They're artists; they're really using and trying to understand the form, not just blathering about themselves. It's easy for people to use sex as a crude and self-congratulatory kind of expression, a signal of hipness. But how could you be an artist and want to communicate without dealing with your own sex and feeling of sexuality?

You said Cézanne makes something spiritual through physical need. It seemed you were yoking, unconsciously perhaps, the making of art with having children. Did your painting change after your son Dakota was born in 1969?

> Yes, radically. For the first time, I realized I was going to die and I was responsible for another life. I think men experience this as well. Along with this sense of being able to give love to someone came this incredible anxiety that I really wanted something for myself too. While I couldn't work the way I wanted to, I realized how much I wanted to be an artist for myself. It wasn't that I felt I was a genius and I had this to

offer to the world. I'm very competitive, but I think that notion of genius is a real male drama. Previously, I took my work for granted; even though I had a full-time job, I could still come home and work at night. With a child, I couldn't do that any more.

Isn't that when you started to draw again?

Yes. I also started to paint again. It took a couple of years before the sculpture dwindled to a stop, and I was pretty miserable. I felt I had to make a radical change, to force myself to do something I didn't want to do. The first thing I did was return to oil paint and I began to get rid of all the images I had used. I felt I had to start with nothing. I never before tried to think about painting without having an image, but I felt the image was getting in the way of the paint. I wanted to get right down to the paint. No apples, just down to the paint as the thing.

And does oil paint have a specific feel?

There's nothing like it. You can build it up; it has a fullness, a depth and a range. At the same time, it can be worked together so it's always one thing.

Let's talk a bit about process. How many paintings do you make each year?

About a dozen. I can't work on more than two at a time.

By not having a backlog of shapes or stretchers, each painting reflects a specific set of moments and reactions. How do you begin?

I draw the shapes on huge pieces of paper, exactly to size. What's exciting is that I draw out the shapes as quickly as I can to keep myself off balance. I try to think about them as little as possible and let them come from unconscious places. I hardly ever re-draw them before I cut them out. It's a way of tricking myself into trying to do or see something that is not so predictable. When the shapes started to get wacky and three-dimensional, I had to get them built in my studio so I could see them because the way the shape comes off the wall and the way the edges are beveled are crucial.

So the drawing becomes like the template?

Yes. There are very simple instructions written on them, like, "ten inches up, this goes in, that goes out." It looks more complicated than it is. For instance, in order to get the beveled edge, we build up layers of plywood in steps, sand the edges smooth, and put a piece of poplar stripping around it. It's like a veneer so it's very flexible and you can get it to bend. It's laminating. My assistants know a lot about carpentry and we try to figure it out together.

This clearly relates to the earlier discussions about sculpture.

Very much so. But if I couldn't afford to have help, I just wouldn't do it; I'd just paint flat. I don't want my work to become something I can't deal with physically. I don't want it to get to an heroic rather than more human scale. Size has a lot to do with how I'm feeling about my body and how I want to put paint down. Do I want to make big motions as opposed to working smaller in a denser, tighter, more contained way? This year I made some small paintings, which took forever to do; it was so hard to switch to working up close. It's like piling food onto a plate and then taking some off again. With large paintings, I don't think about the paint that way because I keep working all over until I begin to hone down special areas. I think a small painting is more intensely introspective, while a larger one is more expansive.

The beveling increases the sense of perspectival retreat as well as the speed or velocity of shape.

It's like another space to paint because the edge makes it possible to slide into another surface.

So you go from the drawing to the manufacturing. Do you know from the drawing where you want the pieces to go?

No, no. Sometimes I'm really not sure how the shapes go. When the frames are done, they get covered with canvas and go up on the wall. In the painting I'm working on now [Open Book] I knew the two big shapes would go together, but I didn't know what to do with the smaller shapes. We put them down on the ground and I just fiddled around; it didn't take too long to figure it out. If something doesn't work, I'll unscrew the pieces and try them other ways.

If mistakes are not irrevocable, have you ever tossed a canvas?

I threw out some this spring because I realized I had done them before. I would have felt I was standing still if I went ahead and worked on them. I can delude myself in some ways but not in that way; I get anxious to discover a new way to paint which brings back the pleasure.

So there is a kind of arranging or composing of parts until you've got the structure of the painting.

Then I start to paint. Initially, I don't want to think about anything. Three days into the process of painting [Open Book], I am thinking about color already; I know I'm going to have greens and browns in there but, basically, I take paint in tubes that are lying around, half empty, and just throw it down. I play around with it for as long as I can stand it.

Is the green derived from that big dark mountain out there? [Upstate New York]

Yes. When I was getting the colors to bring up here, I thought about those greens that I started to get at last summer in the Gga painting. But this painting might not have one green in it when it is done.

The marks don't go to the edge of the shapes at this stage?

I'm careful to keep the marks in the interior until I have more feel for how I want to use the edges. But I really don't want to be that controlling because that inhibits the beginning; it's a process of trying to be unconscious and very deliberate at the same time.

It's putting your control into automatic pilot.

That's a good way of describing it. Starting to make a painting is like starting to tell a story. You build the history. Even though you could question how a first stroke could be so critical, I believe that one thing feeds into another thing. It's a dialectic. To me, that's a metaphor for life.

You've got so many ways of drawing: the beveled outer edge which becomes a sinewy line, the shadowy joint between shapes and the actual strokes which are curiously more linear because of the roundness of the forms on which they occur.

At this point some of the lines automatically take on a shape along the contours. I'm curious if you can see that the two shapes are a book opening, with two pages closing.

Not immediately, but even at this nascent stage it seems like a very lyrical, graceful picture.

I'm suspicious of that part. I'll probably try to combat that.

What does an open book mean to you?

I think it's loaded. I started to think about the image in Her Story which contains a figure with a book in her lap. I thought about Cézanne, and wondered if when men painted books in the laps of women, they were representing genitalia. I realized also that I associated books with my mother. Her Story is really a portrait of her sitting with a book, holding a cup.

Did she read to you?

She read to us and to herself a lot. It is a very tranquil, but also withdrawn image. I confess the idea of a book opening seems very beautiful to me. The sexual context is diffused. It reminds me that the desire to reveal involves the terror of doing so. These paintings involve the viewer in a kind of benign voyeurism. There are even holes in this book, the body of the painting. I'm thinking that inside the book there will be a womb. I don't know if I'll actually do that, but I'm getting less shy about telling people what I'm thinking about. I'm getting less afraid about my ideas and feelings merging. I guess I once felt ideas and feelings were very separate, and I was very suspicious of ideas even though, God knows, I often approach things very intellectually. Now I feel very confident that those things come together, are not separate.

What are the big issues now? If one reaches a point in one's life where the emotions and the intellect are congruent, that's an enormous accomplishment.

With every painting, I have to backtrack to the beginning and travel through the whole process again. I don't start finishing the painting until the moment I begin to hate it, and I almost welcome the feeling because I know I'm finally starting to put the screws on, to get objective. You have to be enormously critical of yourself all the time. I never let go of a painting until it works out. Really, it's not that the painting is worked out but, rather, the experience of making it is completed. And I don't want to see a painting after that; it is too much like the shell of an experience. The difference now is that I feel more whole myself. I feel incredibly lucky that people care about what I've done. If you're lucky enough to keep doing your work, things get worked out. It's just like your life: as you go along, you pull yourself together.

Do you think the broadened definition of abstraction—the sense that abstraction does not preclude stories—makes you comfortable enough to tell people what you're doing?

If I have to claim I am one thing or another, I am an abstract painter. In the 1970s when I came to New York, the definitions of what one could paint and do were closing down. It was a very strict, conceptual scene. I wanted to open up my painting, to be inclusive. I felt I could go against the prevailing trends because Minimalism and Conceptualism weren't part of my character. It really was good for me to have had something to butt my head against because it made it clear how I did not want my work to look.

In your work there's often a melancholic or somber element mixed with the comic, suggesting tragedy and comedy are linked. We've talked about art as being a major pleasure, inspiration, and goad, but what are some of the extra-aesthetic experiences that inform your work?

Clearly, there's a point when the pleasure outweighs the pain. Something keeps you going a little bit more, a little bit more. Once you're lucky enough to hit the pleasurable end, you can't cut yourself off from it. But I think it's true that to

understand things you occasionally have to lose something; that became clear when my mother died. Her death brought home what I wanted my work to be around and about. Paintings like *Can You Hear Me?* or *More Than You Know* were specifically about the experience of being with her when she was dying and the grieving afterwards. I certainly had read great books, seen great films, and looked at great paintings that brought up that experience, but I'd never felt in the middle of that experience or capable of understanding, even expressing, it. I suddenly felt able to realize what I was thinking about.

The first transcendent experience I remember was sitting underneath a huge, golden maple tree in the fall and looking up and seeing the little blue spaces between the leaves. I felt both beauty and sadness; I really wanted to respond to that mix of emotions. I think making art is trying to respond to being alive, to learning about death and how those things mingle. It's what you paint about. That's why people care about it.

Kathy Halbreich
Sue Graze

BIOGRAPHY

1940   Born in Chicago, Illinois

1958–62   Attends The Art Institute of Chicago. Receives B.F.A. in 1962

1962–64   Attends Mills College, Oakland, California. Receives M.F.A. in 1964

1965–67   Instructor, Rosary Hill College, Buffalo, New York

1973   Visiting Artist, Wayne State University, Detroit

1973–74   Visiting Instructor, The Art Institute of Chicago

1974–77   Instructor, Bard College, Annandale-on-Hudson, New York

1975–76   Visiting Instructor, California Institute of the Arts, Valencia, California

1977   Lecturer, Princeton University, New Jersey

1977–80   Instructor, Yale University, New Haven, Connecticut

1978–80   Instructor, School of Visual Arts, New York

1982   Receives Walter M. Campana Award, The Art Institute of Chicago

1986   Receives Skowhegan School of Painting and Sculpture Medal for Painting

SELECTED EXHIBITION HISTORY

Selected exhibition history and bibliography prepared by Elizabeth Simon.

One-Person Exhibitions

1975   Jared Sable Gallery, Toronto, May 24–June 14.

1976   Paula Cooper Gallery, New York, "Elizabeth Murray: Recent Paintings," November 2–27.

1978   The Ohio State University Gallery of Fine Art, Columbus, "Elizabeth Murray Paintings," January 17–31.

Phyllis Kind Gallery, Chicago, "Elizabeth Murray," April 15–May 15.

Paula Cooper Gallery, New York, "Elizabeth Murray: Recent Paintings," October 7–November 4.

1980   Galerie Mukai, Tokyo, February 15–March 15.

Susanne Hilberry Gallery, Birmingham, Michigan, "Elizabeth Murray Paintings and Pastels," May 24–June 22.

1981   Paula Cooper Gallery, New York, "Elizabeth Murray: New Paintings," May 2–30.

1982   Hillyer Gallery, Art Department, Smith College, Northampton, Massachusetts, "Recent Pastels and Prints by Elizabeth Murray, American Artist," April 3–16.

Daniel Weinberg Gallery, Venice, California, "Elizabeth Murray: Recent Paintings and Drawings," September 8–October 9.

1983   Paula Cooper Gallery, New York, "Elizabeth Murray: Paintings," April 2–30.

Portland Center For The Visual Arts, Oregon, "Elizabeth Murray Recent Paintings & Drawings," October 21–November 27.*

1984   Knight Gallery/Spirit Square Arts Center, Charlotte, North Carolina, "Elizabeth Murray Paintings and Drawings," January 27–March 25.*

The Institute of Contemporary Art, Boston, "Currents: Elizabeth Murray," April 10–May 6.*

Paula Cooper Gallery, New York, "Elizabeth Murray," October 2–27.

Brooke Alexander, Inc., New York, "Elizabeth Murray Lithographs 1980–1984," October 20–November 17.

Richard Eugene Fuller Art Gallery, Beaver College, Glenside, Pennsylvania, "Elizabeth Murray Selected Work: Prints, Drawings, Paintings," November 14–December 5.

1985   University Art Museum, The University of New Mexico, Albuquerque, "Elizabeth Murray: Lithographs 1980–1984," October 26–December 15.

1986   Carnegie Mellon University Art Gallery, Pittsburgh, Pennsylvania, "Elizabeth Murray: Drawings 1980–1986," October 25–December 13.*

Selected Group Exhibitions

1972   Whitney Museum of American Art, New York, "1972 Annual Exhibition: Contemporary American Painting," January 25–March 19.*

1973   Whitney Museum of American Art, New York, "1973 Biennial Exhibition: Contemporary American Art," January 10–March 18.*

Whitney Museum of American Art, New York, "American Drawings 1963–1973," May 25–July 22.*

1974   Jacobs Ladder Gallery, Washington, D.C. (with Joseph Zucker), February 9–March 6.

Paula Cooper Gallery, New York, "Marilyn Lenkowsky, Elizabeth Murray, John Torreano," April 6–May 1.

Whitney Museum of American Art, Downtown Branch, New York, "Continuing Abstraction in American Art," September 19–November 1.*

John Doyle Gallery, Cologne, West Germany, "Cologne Kunstmarkt."

Galerie Doyle, Paris, Group Show.

1975   Paula Cooper Gallery, New York, "James Dearing, Elizabeth Murray: Paintings," January 11–February 5.

Michael Walls Gallery, New York, "Thirty Artists in America, Part I," June 7–July 3.

1976   Johnson Gallery, Middlebury College, Middlebury, Vermont, "Recent Work," January 9–30.

Fine Arts Gallery, New York State University College at Brockport, "Recent Abstract Painting," February 8–March 5.*

Hallwalls, Buffalo, New York, "Approaching Painting, Part Three," February 10–March 1.

Paula Cooper Gallery, New York, Group Exhibition, February 14–March 4.

Paula Cooper Gallery, Los Angeles, Changing Group Exhibition, May 25–June 15.

Fine Arts Gallery, California State University, Los Angeles, "New Work/New York," October 4–28.*

*A catalogue or brochure accompanied the exhibition.

Susanne Hilberry Gallery, Birmingham, Michigan, "Opening Exhibition," December 10, 1976–January 15, 1977.

1977 Whitney Museum of American Art, New York, "1977 Biennial Exhibition," February 15–April 3.*

Sarah Lawrence Gallery, Bronxville, New York, "Painting 75 76 77," February 19–March 10, April 2–20 (traveled to the American Foundation for the Arts, Miami, April–July and The Contemporary Arts Center, Cincinnati, Ohio, August–September).*

The Solomon R. Guggenheim Museum, New York, "Nine Artists: Theodoron Awards," March 4–April 7.*

Paula Cooper Gallery, New York, "Group Exhibition," September 10–October 12.

Museum of Contemporary Art, Chicago, "A View of a Decade," September 10–November 10.*

Rhode Island School of Design and Brown University, Providence, "Space Window," September 14–October 6.*

The New York State Museum, Albany, "New York: The State of Art," October 8–November 27.*

The New Museum, New York, "Early Work by Five Contemporary Artists," November 11–December 30.*

The Joe and Emily Lowe Art Gallery, Syracuse University, Syracuse, and Munson-Williams-Proctor Institute, Utica, New York, "Critics' Choice," November 13–December 11, 1977 (Syracuse), January 3–30, 1978 (Utica).*

1978 University of South Florida Art Galleries, Tampa, "Two Decades of Abstraction: New Abstraction," January 8–February 17.*

Institute of Contemporary Art, University of Pennsylvania, Philadelphia, "Eight Abstract Painters," March 18–May 2.*

Paula Cooper Gallery, New York, "Tenth Anniversary Group Exhibition," September 9– October 4.

The Renaissance Society at the University of Chicago, "Thick Paint," October 1–November 8.*

1979 State University of New York at Albany, "Faculty Choice," January 20–February 18.*

Whitney Museum of American Art, New York, "1979 Biennial Exhibition," February 6–April 8.*

Phyllis Kind Gallery, Chicago, "Works on Paper."

Hayward Gallery, Arts Council of Great Britain, London, "New Painting/New York," May 3–June 17.*

Whitney Museum of American Art, New York, "The Decade in Review: Selections from the 1970s," June 19–September 3.*

Grey Art Gallery, New York University, New York, "American Painting: The Eighties," September 5–October 13.*

Paula Cooper Gallery, New York, Group Exhibition, September 8–October 10.

The Ben Shahn Gallery, The William Paterson College, Wayne, New Jersey, "Some Abstract Paintings," Fall.*

Weatherspoon Art Gallery, The University of North Carolina, Greensboro, "Art on Paper 1979," November 11–December 16.*

1980 Galerie Yvon Lambert, Paris, "Paula Cooper at Yvon Lambert," February 16–March 15.

University of Colorado Art Galleries, Boulder, "Selections from a Colorado Collection," March 10–30.

Milwaukee Art Museum, Wisconsin, "Art in Our Time: HHK Foundation for Contemporary Art Inc.," October 9–November 30 (traveled to the Contemporary Arts Center, Cincinnati, Ohio, January 15–March 15, 1981; Columbus Museum of Art, Ohio, June 6–July 19, 1981; Virginia Museum of Fine Arts, Richmond, September 1–October 11, 1981; Krannert Art Museum, University of Illinois, Champaign, November 15–December 31, 1981; High Museum of Art, Atlanta, January 23–March 7, 1982; University of Iowa Museum of Art, Iowa City, April 4–May 31, 1982; Brooks Memorial Art Gallery, Memphis, Tennessee, July 8–September 5, 1982; and the University Art Museum, University of Texas, Austin, November 5–December 19, 1982).*

The Brooklyn Museum, New York, "American Drawing In Black & White: 1970–1980," November 22, 1980–January 18, 1981.*

1981 Oscarsson Hood Gallery, New York, "The 1981 Painting Invitational," January 6–31.

Whitney Museum of American Art, New York, "1981 Biennial Exhibition," January 20–April 19.*

Dart Gallery, Chicago, "Group Show" (curated by Michael Hurson), February 6–March 6.

Galerie Mukai, Tokyo, "Drawings," April 16–May 15.

The High Museum of Art, Atlanta, "Drawings from Georgia Collections 19th & 20th Centuries," May 14–June 28.*

The Contemporary Arts Center, Cincinnati, Ohio, "The RSM Collection," June 3–July 19.*

University Gallery, University of Massachusetts at Amherst, "Selections from the Chase Manhattan Bank Art Collection," September 19–December 20 (traveled to Robert Hull Fleming Museum, University of Vermont at Burlington, January 22–March 21, 1982; and David Winton Bell Gallery, Brown University, Providence, Rhode Island, October 16–November 11, 1982).*

Otis Art Institute of Parsons School of Design, Los Angeles, "Paintings By," September 25–October 18.

Haus der Kunst, Munich, West Germany, "Amerikanische Malerei 1930–1980," November 14, 1981–January 31, 1982.*

Museum of Art, Rhode Island School of Design, Providence, "Art for Your Collection XVIII," December 4–13.

Barbara Toll Fine Arts, New York, "Large Format Drawings," December 8, 1981–January 2, 1982.

Jacksonville Art Museum, Florida, "Currents: A New Mannerism," December 11, 1981–January 24, 1982 (traveled to USF Art Galleries, University of South Florida, Tampa, February 12–March 23, May 14–June 17).*

Paula Cooper Gallery, New York, "Works on Paper," December 12, 1981–January 6, 1982.

1982 Milwaukee Art Museum, Wisconsin, "American Prints: 1960–1980," February 5–March 21.*

Museum of Fine Arts, Boston, "A Private Vision: Contemporary Art from the Graham Gund Collection," February 9–April 4.*

Whitney Museum of American Art, Fairfield County, Stamford, Connecticut, "Surveying the Seventies: Selections from the Permanent Collection of the Whitney Museum of American Art," February 12–March 31.*

American Graffiti, Amsterdam, "Jonathan Borofsky, Michael Hurson, Elizabeth Murray," February 20–March 27.

Hamilton Gallery of Contemporary Art, New York, "The Abstract Image," March 5–27.

The Contemporary Arts Center, Cincinnati, Ohio, "Dynamix," March 11–April 17 (traveled to Sullivant Hall Gallery, Ohio State University, Columbus, September 6–October 17; Allen Memorial Art Museum, Oberlin College, Oberlin, Ohio, November 1–21; Butler Institute of American Art, Youngstown, Ohio, December 6, 1982–January 9, 1983; University of Kentucky Art Museum, Lexington, January 15–February 20, 1983; Joslyn Art Museum, Omaha, Nebraska, March 19–May 1, 1983; and Doane Hall Art Gallery, Allegheny College, Meadville, Pennsylvania, May 5–27, 1983).*

Hayden Gallery, Massachusetts Institute of Technology, Cambridge, "Great Big Drawings," April 3–May 2.*

Whitney Museum of American Art, New York, "Abstract Drawings, 1911–1981," May 5–July 11.*

Art Galaxy, New York, "An Exhibition of Abstract Painting," May 18–June 5 (traveled in part to Muhlenberg College, Allentown, Pennsylvania).

The Art Institute of Chicago, "74th American Exhibition," June 12–August 1.*

Brooke Alexander, Inc., New York, "Selected Prints III," September 7–October 2.*

Paula Cooper Gallery, New York, "Group Exhibition: Paintings, Drawings, Sculpture and Prints," December 1, 1982–January 11, 1983.

1983 Paula Cooper Gallery, New York, "A Painting Exhibition," January 18–February 23.

Daniel Weinberg Gallery, Los Angeles and San Francisco, "Drawing Conclusions—A Survey of American Drawings: 1958–1983," January 29–February 26 (Los Angeles), March 9–April 9 (San Francisco).

Hirshhorn Museum and Sculpture Garden, Washington, D.C., "Directions 1983," March 10–May 15.*

Houghton House Gallery, Hobart and William Smith Colleges, Geneva, New York, "Homage to Arthur Dove: 11 Abstract Painters," March 25–April 12.

The Museum of Modern Art, New York, "Some Contemporary Acquisitions: Painting and Sculpture," May 30–October 11.

Whitney Museum of American Art, New York, "Minimalism to Expressionism: Painting and Sculpture Since 1965 from the Permanent Collection," June 2–December 4.*

Two PPG Place, Pittsburgh, Pennsylvania, "New York Painting Today" (A Three Rivers Arts Festival Exhibition), June 8–26.*

The Museum of Modern Art, New York, "Some Contemporary Prints," July 21–September 13.

Williams College Museum of Art, Williamstown, Massachusetts, "The New England Eye: Master American Paintings from New England School, College & University Collections," September 11–November 6.*

Jersey City Museum, New Jersey, "Selected Drawings: An Exhibition of Works by Sixteen Contemporary Artists," September 14–October 15.*

Harborside Industrial Center, Brooklyn, New York, "Terminal New York," September 24–October 30.

The New Museum, New York, "Language, Drama, Source & Vision," October 8–November 27.*

Susanne Hilberry Gallery, Birmingham, Michigan, "Drawings," October 22–December.

The Brooklyn Museum, New York, "The American Artist As Printmaker: 23rd National Print Exhibition," October 28, 1983–January 22, 1984.*

Washburn Gallery, New York, "Connections," November 3–December 23.

Freedman Gallery, Albright College, Reading, Pennsylvania, "A Painting Show: Selections from a Private Collection," November 29, 1983–January 8, 1984.

1984 Cranbrook Academy of Art Museum, Bloomfield Hills, Michigan, "Viewpoint '84: Out of Square," January 31–April 8.*

Center Gallery, Bucknell University, Lewisburg, Pennsylvania, and Sordoni Art Gallery, Wilkes College, Wilkes-Barre, Pennsylvania, "Parasol and Simca: Two Presses/Two Processes," February 3–April 4 (Lewisburg), April 15–May 13 (Wilkes-Barre).*

Barbara Krakow Gallery, Boston, "Form, Color, Surface: Painting About Itself," February 11–March 8.

American Academy and Institute of Arts and Letters, New York, "Painting and Sculpture by Candidates for Art Awards," March 5–April 1.*

La Jolla Museum of Contemporary Art, California (organized by the Whitney Museum of American Art, New York), "American Art Since 1970: Painting, Sculpture, and Drawings from The Collection of the Whitney Museum of American Art, New York," March 10–April 22, 1984 (traveled to Museo Tamayo, Mexico City, May 17–July 29; North Carolina Museum of Art, Raleigh, September 29–November 25; Sheldon Memorial Art Gallery, University of Nebraska, Lincoln, January 12–March 3, 1985; and Center for the Fine Arts, Miami, March 30–May 26, 1985).*

Hillwood Art Gallery, Long Island University, C.W. Post Campus, Greenvale, New York, and Guild Hall Museum, East Hampton, New York, "Artist in the Theater," March 16–April 12 (Greenvale), June 9–July 15 (East Hampton).*

Whitney Museum of American Art, New York, "Five Painters in New York," March 21–June 17.*

Indianapolis Museum of Art, Indiana, "Painting and Sculpture Today 1984," May 1–June 10.*

The Museum of Modern Art, New York, "An International Survey of Recent Painting and Sculpture," May 17–August 19.*

Siegel Contemporary Art, New York, "Invitational Painting Exhibition Part I: Twelve Abstract Painters," June 5–30.

Center Gallery, Bucknell University, Lewisburg, Pennsylvania, and Sordoni Art Gallery, Wilkes College, Wilkes-Barre, Pennsylvania, "Contemporary Perspectives 1984," October 5–November 25, 1984 (Lewisburg), December 9, 1984–January 6, 1985 (Wilkes-Barre).*

Blum Helman Gallery, New York, "Drawings," October 10–November 3.

Margo Leavin Gallery, Los Angeles, "Eccentric Image(s)," October 20–November 24.

Williams Center for the Arts, Lafayette College, Easton, Pennsylvania and Center for the Arts, Muhlenberg College, Allentown, Pennsylvania, "Small Works: New Abstract Painting," November 12–December 14.*

The Museum of Modern Art, New York, "Contemporary Installation," December 4, 1984–May 14, 1985.

Facets Gallery, The Ackland Art Museum, University of North Carolina at Chapel Hill, "Prints: The State of The Art," December 9, 1984–January 13, 1985.

Diane Brown Gallery, New York, "The Success of Failure," December 12, 1984–January 13, 1985.

1985 Paula Cooper Gallery, New York, Group Exhibition, February 2–March 2.

The Hudson River Museum, Yonkers, New York, "A New Beginning: 1968–1978," February 3–May 5.*

Daniel Weinberg Gallery, Los Angeles, "Drawings," February 20–March 16.

Whitney Museum of American Art, New York, "1985 Biennial Exhibition," March 13–June 9.*

Daniel Weinberg Gallery, Los Angeles, "Now and Then: A Selection of Recent and Earlier Paintings," June 1–August 31.

Colby College Museum of Art, Waterville, Maine, Skowhegan School of Painting and Sculpture, "1985 Faculty Exhibition," June 15–August 20.

Mount Holyoke College Art Museum, South Hadley, Massachusetts, "An Architect's Eye: Selections from the Graham Gund Collection," September 5–November 10.*

Pratt Manhattan Center Gallery, New York, and Pratt Institute Gallery, Brooklyn, "Illuminating Color: Four Approaches in Contemporary Painting and Photography," September 9–October 5 (New York), October 16–November 7 (Brooklyn).*

The Brooklyn Museum, New York, "Contemporary American Prints Recent Acquisitions Louis Comfort Tiffany Foundation Purchases," September 27–December 30.*

University Art Museum, University of California, Santa Barbara, "Scapes," October 30–December 15 (traveled to The Art Gallery, University of Hawaii at Manoa, Honolulu, January 26–February 28, 1986).*

The Katonah Gallery, Katonah, New York, "Rethinking the Avant-Garde," November 3, 1985–January 5, 1986.*

The Art Museum, Princeton University, New Jersey, "A Decade of Visual Arts at Princeton: Faculty 1975–1985," November 17, 1985–January 12, 1986.*

The Museum of Modern Art, New York, "Large Drawings," November 28, 1985–April 15, 1986.

Laforet Museum Harajuku, Tokyo, Japan, "Correspondences: New York Art Now," December 20, 1985–January 19, 1986 (traveled to Tochigi Prefectural Museum of Fine Arts, Utsunomiya, February 8–March 23, 1986; and Tazaki Hall Espace Media, Kobe, April 4–May 15, 1986).*

Knight Gallery/Spirit Square Arts Center, Charlotte, North Carolina, "Drawings," December 20, 1985–February 7, 1986.

1986 Museum of Art, Fort Lauderdale, Florida, "An American Renaissance: Painting and Sculpture Since 1940," January 12–March 30.*

Círculo de Bellas Artes, Madrid, "Pintar con Papel," January 23–March 14.*

Whitney Museum of American Art, Fairfield County, Stamford, Connecticut, "Connecticut Collects: American Art Since 1960," January 29–March 26.*

The Brooklyn Museum, New York, "Public and Private: American Prints Today: The 24th National Print Exhibition," February 7–May 5 (traveled to Flint Institute of Arts, Flint, Michigan, July 28–September 7; Rhode Island School of Design, Providence, September 29–November 9; Museum of Art, Carnegie Institute, Pittsburgh, Pennsylvania, December 1, 1986–January 11, 1987; and the Walker Art Center, Minneapolis, February 1–March 22, 1987).*

Delaware Art Museum, Wilmington, "NYC: New Work," March 7–April 27.*

Paula Cooper Gallery, New York, "Group Exhibition: Large Scale Works by Gallery Artists," March 8–29.

New York Studio School Gallery, "Drawing With Respect to Painting II," April 8–May 9.

The Museum of Contemporary Art, Los Angeles, "The Barry Lowen Collection," June 16–August 10, 1986.*

SELECTED BIBLIOGRAPHY

All publications accompanying exhibitions are listed in the exhibition history only.

1974 Gilbert-Rolfe, Jeremy, "John Torreano, Elizabeth Murray, Marilyn Lenkowsky," *Artforum,* Vol. XII, No. 10 (June 1974), p. 70 (review).

1975 Lubell, Ellen, "James Dearing/Elizabeth Murray," *Arts Magazine,* Vol. 49, No. 7 (March 1975), pp. 14–15 (review).

Moore, Alan, "Elizabeth Murray," *Artforum,* Vol. XIII, No. 8 (April 1975), pp. 82–83 (review).

"Painters (Group One)," *Art-Rite Painting,* No. 9 (Spring 1975), pp. 29–34.

1976 Ratcliff, Carter, "The Paint Thickens," *Artforum,* Vol. XIV, No. 10 (June 1976), pp. 43–47.

Russell, John, "Elizabeth Murray," *The New York Times,* November 12, 1976, p. C18 (review).

1977 Lubell, Ellen, "Elizabeth Murray," *Arts Magazine,* Vol. 51, No. 5 (January 1977), p. 36 (review).

Russell, John, "Art: The New Museum Where Small Is Beautiful," *The New York Times,* November 11, 1977, p. C17.

Russell, John, "It Could Have Been a Disaster. But…," *The New York Times,* November 2, 1977, p. C21.

Smith, Roberta, "Elizabeth Murray at Paula Cooper," *Art in America,* Vol. 65, No. 2 (March–April 1977), p. 114 (review).

1978 Artner, Alan, "A painter's lucky stars turned fate in her favor," *Chicago Tribune,* May 5, 1978, sec. 2, p. 11 (review).

Kuspit, Donald B., "Elizabeth Murray's Dandyish Abstraction," *Artforum,* Vol. XVI, No. 6 (February 1978), pp. 28–31.

The Ohio State University Gallery of Fine Art, Columbus, "Invitational Exhibition, Academic Year 1977–1978," from the portfolio *Exhibitions 1977–8,* Columbus: The Ohio State University Gallery of Fine Art, 1978.

1979 Ashbery, John, "The Perennial Biennial," *New York Magazine,* Vol. 12, No. 12, March 19, 1979, pp. 70–71.

Frank, Peter, "Elizabeth Murray," *ARTnews,* Vol. 78, No. 1 (January 1979), pp. 146, 148 (review).

Lampert, Catherine, "New Work/New York," *Artscribe,* No. 17 (April 1979), pp. 42–43.

Lawson, Thomas, "Painting in New York: An Illustrated Guide," *Flash Art,* No. 92–93 (October–November 1979), pp. 4–11.

Morgan, Stuart, "New Work/New York at the Hayward Gallery, Joe Zucker at the Mayor Gallery," *Artscribe* (July 1979), pp. 52–53.

Perrone, Jeff, "Elizabeth Murray," *Artforum,* Vol. XVII, No. 5 (January 1979), pp. 65–66 (review).

Smith, Roberta, "Elizabeth Murray at Paula Cooper," *Art in America,* Vol. 67, No. 2 (March–April 1979), pp. 150–151 (review).

Smith, Roberta, "Portfolio, a Celebration of Women Artists," *Ambiance* (March 1979), pp. 84–87.

Tatransky, Valentin, "Elizabeth Murray," *Arts Magazine,* Vol. 53, No. 5 (January 1979), p. 18 (review).

1980 Colby, Joy Hakanson, "Twisted shapes, with anxiety built in," *The Detroit News,* June 8, 1980, p. 10E (review).

"Elizabeth Murray Exhibit," *The Daily Yomiuri* (Tokyo), February 22, 1980, p. 6A (review).

Mollenkof, Peter, "Elizabeth Murray," *Asahi Evening News* (Tokyo), February 22, 1980, p. 10 (review).

"Picasso: A Symposium," *Art in America,* Vol. 68, No. 10 (December 1980), pp. 9-19, 185, 187.

1981 Collings, Matthew, "Nothing deep," *Artscribe,* No. 30 (August 1981), pp. 26–29.

Deschamps, Madeleine, *La Peinture Américaine: Les mythes et la matière,* Paris: Editions Denoël, 1981.

Knight, Christopher, "The puzzle that group art shows so often pose," *Los Angeles Herald Examiner,* October 4, 1981, p. E9.

La Badie, Donald, "This Stormy Piece Of Art No 'Tempest' In A Teapot," *Memphis Commercial Appeal,* February 14, 1981.

Levin, Kim, "Elizabeth Murray," *The Village Voice,* Vol. XXVI, No. 21, May 20–26, 1981, p. 90 (review).

Murray, Elizabeth, *Notes for Fire and Rain,* New York: Lapp Princess Press, Ltd., 1981.

Murry, Jesse, "Quintet: The Romance of Order and Tension in Five Paintings by Elizabeth Murray," *Arts Magazine,* Vol. 55, No. 9 (May 1981), pp. 102–105.

Perrone, Jeff, "Notes on the Whitney Biennial," *Images & Issues,* Vol. 2, No. 1 (Summer 1981), pp. 46–49.

Phillips, Deborah C., "Elizabeth Murray at Paula Cooper," *Images & Issues,* Vol. 2, No. 2 (Fall 1981), p. 66 (review).

"Prints & Photographs Published 'Elizabeth Murray,'" *The Print Collector's Newsletter,* Vol. XI, No. 6 (January–February 1981), pp. 210–211.

Russell, John, "Art: Exploding Canvases Of Elizabeth Murray," *The New York Times,* May 8, 1981, p. C20 (review).

1982 Brody, Jacqueline, "Elizabeth Murray, Thinking in Print: An Interview," *The Print Collector's Newsletter,* Vol. XIII, No. 3 (July–August 1982), pp. 73–77.

Cohen, Ronny H., "Elizabeth Murray's Colored Space," *Artforum*, Vol. XXI, No. 4 (December 1982), pp. 51–55.

"Elizabeth Murray/Dondi White," *Bomb Magazine*, No. 4 (1982), p. 28.

Fox, Catherine, "A Portrait Of A Painter," *The Atlanta Constitution*, February 8, 1982, pp. B1, 3.

Friedman, Jon R., "The Abstract Image," *Arts Magazine*, Vol. 56, No. 10 (June 1982), p. 4.

Knight, Christopher, "Paintings with a potential for rich complexity," *Los Angeles Herald Examiner*, September 15, 1982, p. C4 (review).

Murray, Elizabeth, *Bomb Magazine*, No. 4 (1982), pp. 64–65.

Nadelman, Cynthia, "New Editions 'Elizabeth Murray,'" *ARTnews*, Vol. 81, No. 7 (September 1982), pp. 76–77.

Pincus, Robert L., "Venice," *Los Angeles Times*, September 17, 1982, pt. VI, p. 9.

"Prints & Photographs Published 'Elizabeth Murray,'" *The Print Collector's Newsletter*, Vol. XIII, No. 4 (September–October 1982), p. 136.

Sofer, Ken, "An Exhibition of Abstract Painting," *ARTnews*, Vol. 81, No. 9 (November 1982), p. 202 (review).

1983   Ashbery, John, "Biennials Bloom in the Spring," *Newsweek*, Vol. C1, No. 16, April 18, 1983, pp. 93–94.

Cohen, Ronny H., "Drawing Now in New York City: The New, Pictorial Image of the Eighties," *Drawing*, Vol. IV, No. 5 (January–February 1983), pp. 97–101.

Eisenman, Stephen F., "Elizabeth Murray," *Arts Magazine*, Vol. 57, No. 10 (June 1983), pp. 45–46 (review).

"Elizabeth Murray," *Bijutsu Techo Monthly Art Magazine* (Japan), Vol. 35, No. 515 (September 1983), p. 28.

"Elizabeth Murray," *Portland Center for The Visual Arts*, newsletter, October–November, 1983.

Fleming, Lee, "Directions 1983," *ARTnews*, Vol. 82, No. 6 (Summer 1983), pp. 79–82.

Glueck, Grace, "Elizabeth Murray," *The New York Times*, April 8, 1983, p. C25 (review).

Hayakawa, Alan R., "Murray stacks puzzle into pleasing abstract," *The Oregonian* (Portland), November 25, 1983, p. 8F.

Howe, Katherine, "Elizabeth Murray at Paula Cooper," *Images & Issues*, Vol. 4, No. 2 (September/October 1983), p. 63 (review).

Madoff, Steven Henry, "A New Generation of Abstract Painters," *ARTnews*, Vol. 82, No. 9 (November 1983), pp. 78–84.

Miller, Bud, "Elizabeth Murray," *Flash Art*, No. 113 (Summer 1983), p. 65 (review).

Rosenthal, Mark, "The Structured Subject in Contemporary Art: Reflections on Works in the Twentieth-Century Galleries," *Philadelphia Museum of Art Bulletin*, Vol. 79, No. 340 (Fall 1983).

Russell, John, "Painting Is Once Again Provocative," *The New York Times*, April 17, 1983, Arts & Leisure, sec. II, pp. 1, 31.

Smith, Roberta, "Healthy Egos," *The Village Voice*, Vol. XXVIII, No. 18, May 3, 1983, p. 100 (review).

Sofer, Ken, "Elizabeth Murray," *ARTnews*, Vol. 82, No. 7 (September 1983), p. 184 (review).

1984   *Art of Our Time The Saatchi Collection*, Book 4, London: Lund Humphries, Ltd., 1984.

Brenson, Michael, "Elizabeth Murray," *The New York Times*, October 19, 1984, p. C32 (review).

Fineberg, Jonathan, "Tracking the avant-garde," *Harvard Magazine* (January–February 1984), pp. 24–35.

Freeman, Phyllis, Eric Himmel, Edith Pavese, and Anne Yarowsky, eds., *New Art*, New York: Harry N. Abrams, Inc., 1984.

Gardner, Paul, "Elizabeth Murray Shapes Up," *ARTnews*, Vol. 83, No. 7 (September 1984), pp. 46–55.

Gibson, Eric, "Spring exhibitions," *The New Criterion*, Vol. 2, No. 10 (June 1984), pp. 69–72.

Glueck, Grace, "At Whitney, 5 New York Painters," *The New York Times*, March 30, 1984, pp. C1, 28 (review).

Maschal, Richard, "Murray's 'Hot' Art Full Of Energy," *The Charlotte Observer* (North Carolina), February 5, 1984, p. 11F (review).

"Prints & Photographs Published 'Elizabeth Murray,'" *The Print Collector's Newsletter*, Vol. XV, No. 3 (July–August 1984), p. 106.

"Prints & Photographs Published 'Elizabeth Murray,'" *The Print Collector's Newsletter*, Vol. XV, No. 4 (September–October 1984), p. 144.

Ratcliff, Carter, "Five Painters in New York," *Vanity Fair*, Vol. 47, No. 3 (March 1984), pp. 20–21 (review).

Robins, Corinne, *The Pluralist Era: American Art 1968–1981*, New York: Harper and Row Publishers, 1984.

Simon, Joan, "Elizabeth Murray ou le mélange des métaphores," *Art Press* (December 1984–January 1985), pp. 16–18.

Simon, Joan, "Mixing Metaphors: Elizabeth Murray," *Art in America*, Vol. 72, No. 4 (April 1984), pp. 140–147.

Smith, Roberta, "Hidden Manias," *The Village Voice*, Vol. XXIX, No. 16, April 17, 1984, p. 95 (review).

Smith, Roberta, "A Three-Sided Argument," *The Village Voice*, Vol. XXIX, No. 44, October 30, 1984, p. 107 (review).

Westfall, Stephen, "Jan Hashey at Barbara Toll," *Art in America*, Vol. 72, No. 10 (December 1984), p. 165.

1985   Brenson, Michael, "The Whitney Biennial—Art's Cutting Edge?" *The New York Times*, March 17, 1985, sec. 2, pp. 1, 24.

Castleman, Riva, *American Impressions: Prints Since Pollock*, New York: Alfred A. Knopf, 1985.

Flam, Jack, "The Museum as Funhouse," *The Wall Street Journal*, March 27, 1985, p. 32.

Gardner, Paul, "When Is a Painting Finished?" *ARTnews*, Vol. 84, No. 9 (November 1985), pp. 89–99.

Glueck, Grace, "Art: Modern Shows Off Some of Best Drawings," *The New York Times*, January 11, 1985, p. C19 (review).

Hughes, Robert, "Careerism and Hype Amidst the Image Haze," *Time Magazine*, Vol. 125, No. 24, June 17, 1985, pp. 78–83.

Larson, Kay, "Keep your eye on art…women in the vanguard," *Harper's Bazaar*, No. 3280 (March 1985), pp. 276–77, 318, 320.

Lucie-Smith, Edward, *American Art Now*, New York: William Morrow and Company, Inc., 1985.

Perrone, Jeff, "Hugging and Tugging," *Arts Magazine*, Vol. 59, No. 6 (February 1985), pp. 74–77.

Perrone, Jeff, "The Salon of 1985," *Arts Magazine*, Vol. 59, No. 10 (June/Summer 1985), pp. 70–73 (review).

Plagens, Peter, "Nine Biennial Notes," *Art in America*, Vol. 73, No. 7 (July 1985), pp. 114–119 (review).

Rose, Barbara, "Portrait of Paula," *Vogue*, Vol. 175, No. 4 (April 1985), pp. 362–367, 410.

Russell, John, "Art: 1985 Biennial Arrives at Whitney," *The New York Times*, March 22, 1985, pp. 17, 22 Weekend (review).

Security Pacific Corporation, Los Angeles, *The Security Pacific Collection, 1970–1985: Selected Works*, 1985.

Sofer, Ken, "Elizabeth Murray," *ARTnews*, Vol. 84, No. 1 (January 1985), p. 139 (review).

1986   Bell, Tiffany, "Drawing With Respect to Painting," *Arts Magazine*, Vol. 60, No. 10 (June/Summer 1986), pp. 123–124 (review).

Brenson, Michael, "Drawing With Respect to Painting," *The New York Times*, May 2, 1986, p. C32 (review).

Larson, Kay, "One from the Heart," *New York Magazine*, Vol. 19, No. 6, February 10, 1986, pp. 40–45.

Storr, Robert, "Added Dimension," *Parkett*, No. 8, 1986, pp. 8–19.

LENDERS TO THE EXHIBITION

Mr. and Mrs. Harry W. Anderson
Harrison Augur
Barbara and Bruce Berger
The Edward R. Broida Trust
Mathieu Carrière
Paula Cooper
Douglas S. Cramer
Dallas Museum of Art
Edward R. Downe, Jr.
Marianne and Jonathan Fineberg
Robert and Gayle Greenhill
Agnes Gund
Robert H. Halff
High Museum of Art
Estée Lauder Cosmetics
Robert K. and Loretta Lifton
Susan and Lewis Manilow
Massachusetts Institute of Technology
Memphis Brooks Museum of Art
Elizabeth Murray
The Museum of Contemporary Art,
    Los Angeles
Museum of Fine Arts, Boston
The Museum of Modern Art
Drs. Steven and Sara Newman
Paul and Camille Oliver-Hoffmann
Mr. Andrew J. Ong
Philadelphia Museum of Art
Saatchi Collection, London
The Saint Louis Art Museum
Security Pacific Corporation
Martin Sklar
Speyer Family Collection
Sari and Rick Swig
Jane M. Timken
Walker Art Center
Wellington Management Company/
    Thorndike, Doran, Paine & Lewis
Whitney Museum of American Art
Private Collections

CATALOGUE
OF THE EXHIBITION

All dimensions are in inches.
Height precedes width precedes depth.

Paintings

Beginner, 1976. Oil on canvas, 113 × 114″.
Saatchi Collection, London

Searchin', 1976–77. Oil on canvas, 51½ × 58¼″.
Collection Edward R. Downe, Jr.

New York Dawn, 1977. Oil on canvas, 88½ × 65″.
Saatchi Collection, London

Spring Point, 1977. Oil on canvas, 48 × 41¾″.
Collection Susan and Lewis Manilow

*__Children Meeting__, 1978. Oil on canvas, 101 × 127″.
Collection Whitney Museum of American Art,
New York; Purchase with funds from the Louis
and Bessie Adler Foundation, Inc.;
Seymour M. Klein, President. 78.34

Tempest, 1979. Oil on canvas, 120 × 170″.
Collection Memphis Brooks Museum of Art,
Memphis, Tennessee; Gift of Art Today,
purchased with matching funds from the
National Endowment for the Arts 80.7

**Writer, 1979. Oil on canvas, 137 × 74½″.
Collection The Saint Louis Art Museum.
Funds given by Mrs. Theodore R. Gamble
and the Contemporary Art Society

Join, 1980. Oil on 2 canvases, 133 × 120″.
Collection Security Pacific Corporation

Breaking, 1980. Oil on 2 canvases, 108 × 108″.
Collection Paul and Camille Oliver-Hoffmann

Brush's Shadow, 1981. Oil on canvas, 116 × 86½″.
Collection High Museum of Art, Atlanta, Georgia;
Gift of Frances Floyd Cocke, 1981.54

Painters' Progress, 1981. Oil on 19 canvases, 116 × 93″.
Collection The Museum of Modern Art, New York,
Acquired through the Bernhill and Agnes Gund
Funds, 1983

Heart and Mind, 1981. Oil on 2 canvases, 111¾ × 114″.
Collection The Museum of Contemporary Art,
Los Angeles: The Barry Lowen Collection

Just in Time, 1981. Oil on 2 canvases, 106½ × 97″.
Collection Philadelphia Museum of Art, Purchase:
The Edward and Althea Budd Fund,
Adele Haas Turner and Beatrice Pastorius Turner
Fund and funds contributed by
Marion Stroud Swingle and Lorine E. Vogt

Bean, 1982. Oil on 3 canvases, 117⅛ × 116″.
Collection of the artist

Yikes, 1982. Oil on 2 canvases, 116 × 113″.
Collection Douglas S. Cramer

Long Arm, 1982. Oil on 7 canvases, 107 × 85″.
Collection Martin Sklar

Keyhole, 1982. Oil on 2 canvases, 99½ × 110½″.
Collection Agnes Gund

Shown at the Whitney Museum of American Art only.
**Shown at the Dallas Museum of Art and MIT only.*

Beam, 1982. Oil on 4 canvases, 110 × 77″.
    Private Collection

Table Turning, 1982–83. Oil on 2 canvases,
    106¼ × 100¼″. Collection of the artist

Sail Baby, 1983. Oil on 3 canvases, 126 × 135″.
    Collection Walker Art Center, Minneapolis;
    Walker Special Purchase Fund

Deeper than D., 1983. Oil on 2 canvases, 106 × 102″.
    Private Collection

More Than You Know, 1983. Oil on 9 canvases,
    108 × 111 × 8″. Collection The Edward R. Broida
    Trust, Los Angeles

Sleep, 1983–84. Oil on canvas, 129 × 129″.
    Saatchi Collection, London

Can You Hear Me?, 1984. Oil on 4 canvases,
    106 × 159 × 12″. Collection Dallas Museum of Art,
    Foundation for the Arts Collection, anonymous gift

Her Story, 1984. Oil on 3 canvases, 105 × 132″.
    Collection Robert K. and Loretta Lifton

Kitchen Painting, 1985. Oil on 2 canvases,
    81 × 58 × 14″. Collection Paula Cooper

Chain Gang, 1985–86. Oil on 4 canvases,
    114½ × 125½ × 16¼″.
    Collection Mr. and Mrs. Harry W. Anderson

Drawings

September, 1979. Charcoal and pastel on paper,
    38¼ × 40¾″. Collection Harrison Augur

Drawing for Fall, 1979. Charcoal and pastel on paper,
    40 × 25¾″. Collection Jane M. Timken

Cup, 1981. Pastel on 3 sheets of paper, 44⅛ × 41⅜″.
    Collection Barbara and Bruce Berger

Painter's Partner II, 1981. Charcoal and pastel on paper,
    52 × 60″. Speyer Family Collection

Painter's Partner III, 1981. Charcoal and pastel on 2
    sheets of paper, 56 × 33″. Collection Marianne
    and Jonathan Fineberg, Urbana, Illinois

Phone II, 1981. Charcoal and pastel on 2 sheets of paper,
    40 × 27⅞″. Collection Museum of Fine Arts,
    Boston, gift of The Charles Z. Offin Art Fund, 1982

Untitled, 1981. Charcoal and pastel on 3 sheets of
    paper, 29½ × 70″. Collection Mr. Andrew J. Ong

Untitled, 1981. Charcoal and pastel on 4 sheets of
    paper, 61¾ × 46″. Collection Paula Cooper

Walk Drawing, 1981. Pastel on paper, 35½ × 52″.
    Private Collection

Popeye, 1982. Pastel and charcoal on 8 sheets of cut-
    and-pasted paper, 76½ × 37¾″.
    Collection The Museum of Modern Art, New York.
    Gift of Abby Aldrich Rockefeller (by exchange)

Hear, 1982. Pastel on 2 sheets of paper, 30½ × 35″.
    Collection Robert H. Halff

Last Night, 1982. Pastel on 8 sheets of paper,
    65½ × 52″. Permanent Collection, Massachusetts
    Institute of Technology

Black Tree, 1982. Pastel on 2 sheets of paper, 48 × 36″.
    Collection Estée Lauder Cosmetics

Sophie Last Summer, 1983. Charcoal and pastel on 5
    sheets of paper, 52⅛ × 26″. Collection of the artist

Untitled, 1984. Pastel on 2 sheets of paper, 35 × 24½″.
    Collection Mathieu Carrière

Untitled, 1984. Charcoal with rubber eraser on paper,
    44 × 30″. Collection Sari and Rick Swig

Palm, 1984. Charcoal and pastel with wood on 5 sheets
    of paper, 59 × 29″. Wellington Management Com-
    pany/Thorndike, Doran, Paine & Lewis Collection

Both Hands, 1984. Charcoal and pastel with clay on 2
    sheets of paper, 17 × 52″.
    Collection Drs. Steven and Sara Newman

Untitled, 1985. Pastel on 2 sheets of paper, 47 × 52¼″.
    Collection Robert and Gayle Greenhill

ACKNOWLEDGMENTS

The pleasures of organizing this exhibition surpass the visual. As in her paintings, Elizabeth Murray was more than generous in her willingness to plumb the personal, to marry autobiography and art. Bob Holman's epigrammatic poem at the beginning of this book reveals his role in this mix; an astute and witty observer of Elizabeth's work, he also is her husband and the father of their two daughters. Clearly, we benefitted from and value the days spent in the midst of both Elizabeth's family and studio. We thank Elizabeth, Bob, Sophie, Daisy, and Dakota for allowing us to join their table and Diana McWilliams for making it possible.

Countless hours were spent in conversation with Paula Cooper and Douglas Baxter whose assistance in securing crucial loans made the ideal possible. Paula Cooper's entire gallery staff answered questions and gathered pertinent materials with speed and cheer; in particular we'd like to thank Steve Wolfe, Kristoffer Haynes, and Carol Caldwell.

Many individuals were committed to the production of this publication. Margaret Kaplan, Senior Vice President and Executive Editor of Harry N. Abrams, believed in this book from the beginning. Edith Pavese, Senior Editor, helped us realize our aspirations. Roberta Smith contributed important insights into the artist's methods and concerns, while Clifford Ackley introduced some salient notes on Murray's drawings. Elizabeth Simon, Curatorial Assistant at the Dallas Museum, displayed extraordinary care in preparing the exhibition history and bibliography contained in this volume. Jennifer Bartlett, Robert Moskowitz, Patterson Sims, and Jenny Snider generously loaned us early paintings to reproduce for Smith's essay, while Margo Leavin allowed us to use her gallery to photograph West Coast work.

Our colleagues at the five other museums hosting this exhibition offered invaluable support. Clifford Ackley, Curator of Prints, Drawings and Photographs of the Museum of Fine Arts, Boston; Richard Koshalek, Director, and Julia Brown Turrell, former Senior Curator of The Museum of Contemporary Art, Los Angeles; David Ryan, former Director, and Peggy Patrick, Acting Director of the Des Moines Art Center; Martin Friedman, Director, and Robert Murdock, former Chief Curator, of the Walker Art Center; Thomas N. Armstrong, III, Director, and Richard Armstrong, Adjunct Curator of the Whitney Museum of American Art were hearty collaborators. Joan Simon was the earliest of supporters.

Closer to home, we appreciated the support and guidance of Harry Parker, Director of the Dallas Museum and Paul Gray, President of Massachusetts Institute of Technology. At the Dallas Museum, Steven Nash, Deputy Director/Chief Curator; Anna McFarland, Associate Curator of Exhibitions, and Irene Martin, former Assistant Chief Curator, worked closely with us. Professor Boris Magasanik, Chairman of the Committee on the Visual Arts at MIT, and Kathryn Lombardi, Executive Assistant to the President, offered important counsel. Jill Aszling, Registrar for the Albert and Vera List Visual Arts Center, oversaw the care of the artist's pastels and paintings while Toby Levi managed the administration of grants, budgets, and personnel; we came to count on both for their grace and efficiency.

The lenders to this exhibition were particularly open-minded given the duration of the tour; we thank each one for helping us realize our aspirations and for allowing Elizabeth's audience to grow. The National Endowment for the Arts and the Massachusetts Council on the Arts and Humanities, enlightened patrons, made the exhibition, publication and tour possible.

Sue Graze
Kathy Halbreich

INDEX TO PLATES

PHOTOGRAPH CREDITS